How Vocaloid Works

Gretchen Jude
Department of Film and Media Arts
University of Utah
Salt Lake City, UT, USA

ISBN 978-3-031-92726-3   ISBN 978-3-031-92727-0 (eBook)
https://doi.org/10.1007/978-3-031-92727-0

© The Author(s) 2025

This work is subject to copyright. All rights are solely and exclusively licensed by the Publisher, whether the whole or part of the material is concerned, specifically the rights of translation, reprinting, reuse of illustrations, recitation, broadcasting, reproduction on microfilms or in any other physical way, and transmission or information storage and retrieval, electronic adaptation, computer software, or by similar or dissimilar methodology now known or hereafter developed.

The use of general descriptive names, registered names, trademarks, service marks, etc. in this publication does not imply, even in the absence of a specific statement, that such names are exempt from the relevant protective laws and regulations and therefore free for general use.

The publisher, the authors and the editors are safe to assume that the advice and information in this book are believed to be true and accurate at the date of publication. Neither the publisher nor the authors or the editors give a warranty, expressed or implied, with respect to the material contained herein or for any errors or omissions that may have been made. The publisher remains neutral with regard to jurisdictional claims in published maps and institutional affiliations.

This Palgrave Macmillan imprint is published by the registered company Springer Nature Switzerland AG.
The registered company address is: Gewerbestrasse 11, 6330 Cham, Switzerland

If disposing of this product, please recycle the paper.

Gretchen Jude

How Vocaloid Works

A Beginner's Guide to the Science Behind Yamaha's
Singing Voice Synthesis Software

Preface

This book stems first from my experience as a composer and performer who uses electronics to alter the sound of my own voice. As a practitioner, understanding the nature and function of my tools is crucial to me. Yet technologies like voice synthesis involve many fields of study, ranging from anatomy to digital signal processing, making it hard to adequately grasp how they work. To further complicate matters, vocal expression, while a human universal, varies almost infinitely—not only between cultures and languages but also according to musical genre and individual style.

In this book, I aim to provide simple yet accurate explanations of the complicated processes and difficult concepts that enable the production of electronically altered and synthesized vocal sound. This includes offering extensive references to pertinent credible sources. The book traces the fascinating quest to synthesize singing, serving as a map indicating many directions. Having lived between Japan and the United States since the late 1990s (studying several lineages of Japanese traditional genres and instruments including koto, shamisen, and voice), I find both the technical and cultural aspects of the Vocaloid phenomenon deeply resonant. Thus, the contributions of Japanese scientists and musicians are central to this book.

As this work will make clear, the history of science and technology is inseparable from the history of art and aesthetics. Especially in the world of music, the ways that we listen to and create sounds are increasingly intertwined with electrical devices and networks. Yet as a singer, I remain acutely aware of the voice's inescapable physicality. Making sound with one's voice engages the body's core muscles and is intimately tied to the very source of life—breath. By contrast, while sounding with machines involves at least one body, the process feels less visceral and requires less physical effort. With audio technology, the power needed to vibrate the air to produce sound comes from the electrical current running the system. Many beings across time and distance have been contributed to the creation of the machines, the code, and the electrical grid. And many more may be involved in listening to the sound created with machines, including future generations—and even us listening to voices long gone or far distant.

These complexities can obscure our understanding of the processes involved in synthesizing a voice. Without a technical grasp of how synthesized singing works, cultural analysis of the intersection of machine and voice can easily stray into ungrounded speculation and abstracted metaphor. My hope is that the book will help to ground useful conversations about the human-like machine voices that are becoming an ever more common part of our auditory landscape.

Finally, while it is not difficult to find 'live' concert footage of Vocaloid avatars such as Hatsune Miku, media documentation of any event misses the fine details of what it is like being there in person. My experience of the Miku Expo 2016 Tour was foundational to my writing about Vocaloid.

Salt Lake City, UT, USA   Gretchen Jude

Acknowledgments

I would like to extend heartfelt thanks to duskin drum for his insightful feedback and engaging conversations on drafts. Thanks also to Conner Lacy, for his reassuring technical expertise and friendship.

I am deeply grateful to my dissertation committee—Henry Spiller, Lynette Hunter, and Ted Apel—for their expert guidance through the weedy chapter that eventually grew into this book. Special thanks go to Lynette, who introduced me to Hatsune Miku over a decade ago!

Endless gratitude and respect for John Bischoff and Molly Holm, whose mentorship in the realms of electronics and voice has shaped my musical thinking and creativity to this day. I am also thankful for my creative collaboration with Arjun Mendiratta in our duo, glou glou—which was both enriching and super fun.

Infinite respect to the transnational Vocaloid community. Your dedication, passion, precision, and generosity continue to inspire and energize me. Online sites like Fandom's *VOCALOID Wiki* and in-person fan events deepened my understanding and interest. I hope this book does justice to the vibrant worlds you continue to create.

All research, writing, and original ideas are solely my own, as are any errors herein.

My Miku Experience

Tuesday, the 29th of March 2016, at Zepp Namba in Osaka: I'm finally going to see Hatsune Miku live in concert! J and I arrive around 6:40pm, stand in a line that snakes halfway around the block but moves incredibly fast. This is an extremely well-oiled machine that we are entering. The thrill of the crowd is palpable as hundreds stream in, skillfully directed by venue workers in navy suits and white gloves. We enter the concert hall just before 7:00pm, and though it is a full house, the Japanese crowd automatically makes room. Once inside the first thing I notice is how conventional the audience looks, clad in dark jackets and tidy unmarked sweatshirts.

The bass booms massively with the intro to the first song. The crowd's energy surges, but there is no pushing toward the stage. I stand by the door, near a venue employee who appears to doze on his short pedestal. There is no unruly behavior for the bouncers to deal with. Which is just as well, since the venue is packed with its capacity of 2500—mostly strait-laced 30-something Japanese men on the standing-room floor, but a few families chaperoning young girls up in the balcony seats. Standing on the first level, I don't get the best view of the stage and feel sorry for the Japanese women at the back. A massive bassline shakes the room as intro comes in—the energy of the crowd surges, but still no push toward the stage. A glimpse of sky-blue ponytail swishing as the star of the show appears, holographically rendered life-sized on a translucent, back-lit screen.

Miku dances a routine that many obviously know from various videos and games, while for other songs, she appears with a mic or guitar in hand. Her human band members are a surprisingly important part of the show. The keyboard player Meg.Me in particular draws my eye, since she is on a pedestal above the guitarist, which puts her directly in my line of sight. I stand on tiptoe and crane my neck to see her dancing above the audience's hand-held wands waving in synchrony. Fans shift their wand colors to represent different Vocaloid character vocals, all six of whom make guest appearances: Miku, Kagamine Rin & Len (paired 'female' and 'male' voicebanks modeled on the donor voice), Megurine Luka, and Kaito and Meiko (updates of Yamaha's original prototypes).

For a moment, the crowd in front of me opens, and I get a clear line of vision straight at Miku and the dark, glassy surface that envelops her. It faintly reflects the crowd, mirrors us back in a sea of waving wands, phosphorescent like deep-sea creatures. This is nothing like watching the scene on a TV screen at home. As with any other show, the crowd creates its own immersive intensity. Miku spins around, disappears from her translucent screen in swirling clouds of smoke or pixelated mist, then reconstitutes from a cloud of light. The swirling patterns of light projected on the ceiling and walls of the cavernous venue reinforce the illusion that we too are part of her ephemeral world, with the performers' projection screen just a veil, a soap bubble between us and the fantasy realm from which Miku and her cohort beckon.

The weirdest moment is when Miku addresses the crowd directly—and everyone, including me, instinctively responds. I feel the strangest sensation of having engaged with a 'real person.' But what this means to me seems something entirely different now. What is it about this so-called future sound—about my listening to it, a human-created nonhuman 'voice'—that produces the impression of hearing an impossible, yet impossibly 'human' voice 'singing'?

Contents

1 Hearing Voices: Human Sound, Aural Perception, and Early Voice Synthesis   1

2 Out of the Analog Age: Singing Robots and the Uncanny Valley   21

3 From Daisy to Miku: Digital Voices in the Information Age   41

4 Future Voices to Come: AI Singing After Miku   63

Index   87

CHAPTER 1

Hearing Voices: Human Sound, Aural Perception, and Early Voice Synthesis

Abstract This chapter begins with a brief overview of Hatsune Miku, Yamaha's most well-known Vocaloid product. A fan-created song from 2014 is examined as a case study, to explore how we recognize and understand human singing. Next, the chapter offers practical definitions of 'voice' as a foundation for understanding singing voice synthesis. It provides an overview of the physiology of vocalization and hearing, covering the basics of phonation, resonance, and articulation, including the distinction between harmonics and formants. Additionally, it describes the auditory system, touching on aural effects such as loudness constancy and perceptual completion. The chapter also delves into several historical efforts to understand human utterance through both physical and perceptual models. The primary physical model of voice discussed is Kempelen's remarkable eighteenth-century Speaking Mechanism, which mechanically synthesized vocal sounds. Helmholtz's groundbreaking work on acoustic resonance and auditory perception in the nineteenth century introduces the perceptual approach, with Helmholtz resonators and tuning forks illustrating the basic concepts of analysis and synthesis of complex waveforms from sinusoids. The chapter introduces key concepts such as frequency and pitch, and includes a brief discussion on the distinctions between speech and singing. Throughout, the chapter emphasizes that the production and perception of voice are both inextricably linked and deeply embodied.

© The Author(s), under exclusive license to Springer Nature Switzerland AG 2025
G. Jude, *How Vocaloid Works*,
https://doi.org/10.1007/978-3-031-92727-0_1

Keywords Hatsune Miku phenomenon • cosMo@Bousou-P • Yuzuki Yukari • Singing voice synthesis (SVS) • Human vocalization • Kempelen's Speaking Mechanism • Helmholtz resonators • Auditory perception • Formant frequencies

1.1 Hatsune Miku and Beyond: Back to the Future

1.1.1 Introducing Future's First Sound

The blue-haired, anime-style image of Hatsune Miku is the iconic face of Yamaha's Vocaloid singing synthesis software. Auspiciously named "first sound of the future," Miku captured the imaginations of audiences and creators alike. Released in 2007, the Hatsune Miku Character Vocal made the Vocaloid synthesis engine a hugely profitable software. In terms of global cultural and economic impact, Miku represents the culmination of a centuries-long quest to build a machine capable of independent utterances: beyond the recording or broadcasting of existing humans voices, but instead an original synthetic vocal sound—one that seems human but is entirely artificial in origin. For Yamaha, Miku was the profitable outcome of an international research project inaugurated in 2000.

Licensed and marketed by Crypton Future Media, Hatsune Miku was the first Vocaloid product released with an illustrated image and persona, including 'her' age (16 years), height (158 centimeters), and weight (42 kilos). Although the initial Vocaloid products, garnering positive reviews, went on sale from 2004, the added visual and character component made all the difference of viral commercial success. By 2008, the synergy between the Vocaloid and NicoNico Douga[1] (a Japanese online media-sharing platform similar to YouTube) pushed music by Vocaloid users, called producers (or 'p') to the top of Japan's pop charts (Takahashi 2011). A year later, an all-Vocaloid compilation album outsold popular foreign import Justin Bieber (Yang 2011). Japanese writers took notice, with one group of researchers calling the synergistic phenomenon "massively collaborative creation via the Web" (Hamasaki et al. 2009: 222).

By 2011 the Hatsune Miku phenomenon was going global (Yang 2011). Miku's U.S. premier at Nokia Theater in Los Angeles sold out a 4000-seat show in July of that year. Cultural anthropologist Ian Condry,

---

[1] Rebranded as Niconico Inc. in 2012.

who was in attendance, gave voice to the excitement many were feeling about this new phenomenon: "Miku hints at a world of untapped possibility, a model of crowd-sourced mobilization, and an instructive instance of a media platform that is part software technology (Vocaloid) part cultural idea (the character Miku)" (Condry 2011). Thanks to Miku, Yamaha's Vocaloid burst into the American media mainstream in 2014. That May, a holographic Hatsune Miku projection 'performed' as Lady Gaga's opening act on her North American tour (Kitamura 2014: 22–23). In October of 2014, digital Miku took the stage with its (all-human) backup band on Late Night with David Letterman. The virtual diva seemed poised to take over the pop world.

Looking back on this time it is clear that Hatsune Miku is now part of a global celebrity pantheon, even meriting a seminar at Japan's premier institution, University of Tokyo, which kicked off in 2016 (Ayukawa 2022). Despite remaining forever sixteen, Miku is no longer on the cutting edge. Yet the unique synthesized qualities of Miku's 'voice' remain recognizable as 'hers'—a famously virtual artifice capable of resembling the vocalization of an organic, embodied human being. In other words, the world's first commercially successful synthesized singing voice.

1.1.2 Hearing Singing: A 'Magic' Combination

Suetsugu (2013) describes the respect accorded to Vocaloid producers who can create "close-to-natural" vocals, observing that the skill is referred to as *kamichōkyō* [divine training] (Suetsugu 2013: 54, my translation). However, rather than aspiring to the "supernatural" ability described by Suetsugu (2013 54 my translation), other popular Japanese producers explore the possibilities of Yamaha's singing synthesis technology by highlighting the quirky, nonhuman sounds of the software, featuring musical feats nearly impossible for humans to vocalize. The fast tempo of songs by producers like cosMo@Bousou-P's 2008 release "The End of Hatsune Miku—Dead End"[2] ([Official] THE END 2018) and "The Intense Voice of Hatsune Miku"[3] ([Official] The Intense 2018) from 2010 speed up lyrics and melody lines to the extreme limit of comprehensibility. In response, fans and Internet personalities record these songs as karaoke performances, attempting to meet the physical challenge of these songs,

---

[2] *Hatsune Miku no Shōshitsu Kanren.*
[3] *Hatsune Miku no Gekishō.*

illustrating one aspect of the collaborative creativity that is a hallmark of the Vocaloid phenomenon. Nijiro Zamurai (The Disappearance 2023) and nory (Hatsune 2021) exhibit levels virtuosity (which in the latter example seems to include use of pitch correction) while Ganmendoshakuzure (Ningen 2021) takes a more humorous approach.

Vocaloid producer kyaami, in her 2014 cover of a Japanese ballad called "Mahō" [Magic], clearly dedicated hours of detailed work at the onscreen software controls (such as a keyboard roll input for melody, lyrics for pronunciation, and performance expression instructions), taking Suetsugu's "god-in-training" approach to her use of the synthesis software to closely mimic an organic human voice. As listeners' comments[4] indicate, the vocals closely resemble recordings of a skilled human singer (Yuzuki 2014). Originally released by Fullkawa Honpo[5] with singer Chomaiyo in 2012, the "Mahō" cover was edited by kyaami using the 2011 Yuzuki Yukari voicebank, which was produced by Vocalomakets and marketed by AH Software for Yamaha's Vocaloid 3 synthesis engine. Kyaami credits umberellaguns with the UST (User-created Synchronization Track)—file containing the song's lyrics and melody—another example of the deeply collaborative nature of the Vocaloid fan community. The producer uses well-timed (and purposefully audible) in-breath sounds at the onset of each line of the melody. The timing of melody's pitch glides also sounds convincingly organic. Subtle shifts in volume give these scoops and glissandi a natural weight, as if the sung words were emerging on the breath with varying support from the diaphragm. Consonants that sound slightly unusual turn out to be close approximations of (human) singer Chomaiyo's idiosyncratic pronunciation.

If I hadn't listened to kyaami's cover with the foreknowledge of the singer being Vocaloid, I would assume the recording was sung by a human. The acoustic guitar accompaniment (provided by sm19332610) and the

---

[4] The song has received very positive comments over the years: *I don't know what kind of Mahou you use, (snicker snicker) but the tears are streaming down listening to the prefect vibrato. And the consonants. And the spot on mixing. You have made lot's [sic] of vocaloid snobs weep in beauty* (user marygraceboronski1235). *The first time i heard this, first thought that passed on my head are "who is the singer?" After i re read some comments, imagine my surprise that this is vocaloid* (user yan7947) and *You make her sound so real, and her voice has so much feeling! I showed this to my friends, and they all thought it was a real person before I told them it was a Vocaloid* (user KawanoMino21).

[5] An established Vocaloid producer under the name of Fullkawa-P from 2009, he branched out into live vocal performance in 2011.

emotional content of the genre and lyrics match the vocal style, emphasizing the 'humanness' of this Vocaloid rendition. More generally, the success of this illusion also relies on my recognition of a voice-like sound emerging from a black box called a speaker and my tacit acceptance of that sound as a person singing. Kyaami's "Mahō" was created by a human, but at no point did the vocals in the track emerge from a human body. To understand how digital tools can produce convincingly human-sounding singing synthesis, it is essential to grasp the basics of human vocal sound and auditory perception. How exactly did we get here?

1.2 How Does a Voice Sound?

1.2.1 What Is Singing Voice Synthesis?

By definition, singing synthesis aims not to reproduce an existing voice (as with analog and digital playback technologies) but to artificially create facsimiles of musical utterances by a human voice. Signal processing engineer, acoustician, and experimental composer Joseph P. Olive observes that voice synthesis means vocals can be "generated algorithmically by a set of rules rather than reproducing previous (recorded) utterances" (Olive 1998: 111). Synthesis is generally understood to require electronic technologies, but scientists have been devising mechanical models to create the sound of voice without human vocalization since the eighteenth century.

The term 'voice' refers to concepts far beyond its most literal meaning—which is unsurprising since vocalizing is a fundamental part of human existence starting with a newborn infant's cry following its first breath. Voice engenders metaphors for interpersonal communication, self-expression, political power, and even metaphysical existence. The voice is used for communication and expression in song and speech of abstract meaning and emotion, with some scholars postulating the concurrent development of the two, with singing possibly even predating speech (Scherer 2019). Most concretely and simply put, 'voice' denotes sound produced by a human's vocal folds and resonated by the cavities of head and throat.

1.2.2   Phonation: Vocal Vibrations

Vocalization is a complex process beginning with phonation—the vibration of the vocal folds. The vocal folds (or vocal cords) are two folded lengths of mucosal soft tissue attached via cartilage to a complex set of tiny muscles and ligaments of the larynx (or voice box). Breath comes in and out of the lungs through the trachea (or windpipe) below the larynx. As the thumbnail-sized vocal folds open for the breath to move or close the windpipe for swallowing, they form a space between them called the glottis (Titze 2008). The movement of the glottis is fundamental not only for breathing and eating but also for coughing and stabilizing the torso. For instance, when lifting a heavy object, closing the glottis traps the volume of air held in the lungs and helps solidify the core of the body. Phonation engages all the parts of the body involved in breathing: the lungs and diaphragm, as well as the muscles of the abdomen, chest, and back (Dayme 2005; Maragos 2015).

To vocalize, breath moves in and out in a smooth stream; the larynx holds the vocal folds in a balance of tension and relaxation that allows them to oscillate together and apart rapidly enough to produce audible vibrations in the air (or soundwaves). The pitch and loudness of the sound emerging from the larynx changes with the tension on the vocal folds, as they vibrate faster or slower (higher or lower pitch), and with more or less force (louder or quieter). Intricate coordination of these movements by the nervous system allows humans to learn to automatically perform the complex set of movements required for phonation (Dayme 2005; Jiang 2015).

The automaticity of these movements obscures the subtlety and economy of their design. The muscles of the larynx do not themselves directly drive each oscillation, but instead rely on the laws of physics, specifically aerodynamics, to maintain rapid vibration of the vocal folds in what is called the glottal cycle. When the glottis is closed, it traps air in the lungs, releasing the air when it opens to release the increased air pressure. With the release of air pressure, the vocal folds quickly close again. Once this cycle of rapid opening and closing is initiated, the vocal folds' oscillation between open and closed is maintained through a balance of tension and elasticity as the biomechanical properties of the vocal folds direct air pressure differences for a smooth and continuous vibration (Jiang 40–45). The vibration of human vocal folds averages at a frequency of between 110 and 300 Hertz (vibratory cycles per second), depending on the size and thickness of the vocal folds. Not only a slower rate of vibration but also thicker vocal folds result in a lower pitch.

The small, quick bursts of air released through glottis result in a sound commonly described as the glottal wave (or pulse wave). Increasing and decreasing the tension of the vocal folds using the laryngeal muscles moves the frequency of the pulse wave up and down, so the pitch of the glottal wave can move higher and lower. A three-layer structure of the vocal fold tissue allows human vocalization, which normally occurs within a two-octave range, to expand up to five octaves in vocalization by trained singers (Titze 2008).

1.2.3 Harmonics and Resonance

The glottal wave is a small and buzzy sound which must resonate inside the body before it emerges with the sonic characteristics of a human voice. Resonance means that an object or cavity, when exposed to a vibration, vibrates along in accordance with the object's own material qualities, amplifying (increasing the power of) the original vibration. A resonating body or chamber amplifies some frequencies more than others, thus contributing to the timbre of the original sound.

In the case of the human voice, what resonates the vocal folds' glottal wave is the vocal tract, which consists of the pharynx (the tube running from the back of the nose down to the larynx and esophagus) and mouth. As a mobile cavity, the vocal tract amplifies the frequency content of the glottal wave differently, depending on its changing length and shape (Dayme 2005; Titze 2008).

Frequency, measured in Hertz (Hz), refers to how many times per second the object vibrates. A pitched sound, like a musical note, has a periodic oscillation, meaning it repeats at regular intervals. The primary frequency, called the fundamental frequency, is what we perceive as the sound's pitch.[6] Along with the fundamental, higher-frequency vibrations (called harmonics or overtones) occur as integer (whole-number) multiples of the fundamental frequency. The specific harmonics present, as well as their relative amplitude (loudness), determine the timbre of a tone.

---

[6] Pitch perception depends on periodicity but differs from the measure of frequency in some significant ways, most famously in the phenomenon of the missing fundamental. For further reading, see Cheveigné (2010).

When the tiny vocal folds stretch and vibrate in the exhaled stream of breath coming from the lungs, they produce sound at a fundamental frequency (F0) along with harmonics, the overall proportion of which changes depending on the tension of the folds. This rich vibration results from the physical properties of the vocal folds. As the vibration passes through the vocal tract, some harmonics are amplified (made louder) as they resonate according to the physical qualities, shapes, and airflow of the vocal tract (Titze 2008).

1.2.4 Articulation: Shaping Sound into Speech and Song

In addition to the harmonic resonance of the voice, which functions like other musical instruments, the vocal tract also creates special peaks in resonance called formant frequencies. Formants change depending on the shape and configuration of the vocal tract, within specific patterns that reflect human physiology. Since formants come from the resonant features of the vocal tract, they do not vibrate in a fixed mathematical ratio to the fundamental frequency of the vocal cord vibration like harmonic resonances. Instead, formants cluster in frequency bands depending on the position of the jaw, lips, and tongue—the articulators that shape the sounds of language. These formant frequencies are what makes us able to create and distinguish between the vowel sounds 'oo,' 'ee,' and 'ah,' for example, regardless of the fundamental frequency of the phonation. Several measurable formant bands can be measured, with the frequencies of the two lowest formants (F1 and F2) determining the vowels we hear (Sundberg 2019: 127).

Additional articulators in the vocal tract are crucial in producing consonants, which involves moving not only the tongue and lips but also the velum (soft palate) in relation to hard parts of the vocal tract (teeth and hard palate). Consonant production involves constricting or stopping the airflow (as well as redirecting it to exit through the nasal cavity rather than the mouth). The specific sounds of these articulations depend on the language, but they often entail adding (or substituting) random noise energy to (or for) pitched sound. Linguists categorize consonants into two general types: voiced, meaning that the glottis vibrates to produce sound concurrently with the mouth motion, and voiceless, indicating no phonation as the consonant is pronounced (Dayme 2005; Cook 1999a). For example, the English 'f' and 'p' sounds in the word 'fop' are both voiceless consonants, whereas the 'g' and 'd' sounds in the word 'god' are both voiced consonants.

All articulators are used in both speaking and singing, but there is a distinction in the patterns of articulation between these modes of vocalization. In most cultural contexts, the vocal characteristics of speech and singing diverge significantly, with singing requiring longer breath to sustain musical phrases and greater variations in pitch (Sundberg 2019: 118–119). Although intonation and pitched tones may be part of a language's meaning-making systems such as prosody, syntax, or phonology, a singing voice primarily produces melody and precise pitch within a musical system, rather than within a linguistic one; comprehensibility of a song's lyrics is secondary in some genres, and many songs exist without words altogether. While phonation is the basis of both speech and singing, singing typically involves much more continuous glottal vibration (primarily through vowels), whereas speech includes a significant amount of consonant articulation, which can account for up to 40% of spoken utterances (Cook 1999b: 139). Knowing the importance of vowels and consonants to both singing and speaking, we can clarify our definition of voice to include them: sound created by a human's breath vibrating vocal folds, resonated by the cavities of head and throat and shaped by the articulatory system to form consonants and vowels.

1.3 Early Models of Vocal Sound: From Production to Perception

1.3.1 Kempelen's Speaking Mechanism

Current scientific understanding about the human voice developed in tandem with attempts to mechanically mimic vocal sound starting in the late eighteenth century. In 1780, Christian Gottlieb Kratzenstein (1723–1795), a German physician and engineer, submitted a report on the nature of vowels to a Russian scientific competition, along with his plan for a pipe organ with five tubes shaped to produce the sounds a, e, i, o, and u when blown through (Lindsay 1997; Brackhane 2015; Story 2019). Kratzenstein inaccurately theorized that the voice was a wind instrument, with the source of human vocal sound being the epiglottis (the flap of cartilage covering the trachea that protects the lungs from food or liquids entering the lungs) rather than the varying vibrations of the vocal cords as was later discovered (Brackhane 2015). Unfortunately, neither the instrument prototype nor any illustration or precise description remains (Brackhane 2015), but Kratzenstein's contemporaries described it as "a very important discovery" which had the potential to help people "'whose voice is either too weak or disagreeable'" (Euler, qtd. in Story 2019: 11).

Just three years later, Hungarian inventor Wolfgang von Kempelen (1734–1804) introduced his own mechanical analog of a vocal tract. Kempelen, like many who followed him, modeled the vocal tract as sequential cylindrical acoustic tubes. Furthermore, he based his machine on empirical evidence on the functioning of the human voice, whereas Kratzenstein, who painstakingly followed the philosophical approach still common in his time, proceeded with his theories without anatomical observation (Brackhane 2015). As history shows, the empirical approach has proved more productive than philosophy alone, as Kempelen aimed to actually create a physical model to synthesize human voice.

Kempelen's mechanical voice instrument had been in development since around 1769, when he first attempted to synthesize vowels. Once Kempelen built his device, he toured with what he called his "Mechanism" across Europe from 1783 to 1784, publishing the results of his vowel study in 1791 (Kempelen 1791/2017). As Brackhane (2017) describes, the speaking machine was a playable instrument whose design shows nascent empirical knowledge of the vocal apparatus:

> [T]he machine's construction represents an extensive modeling of human anatomy, insofar as necessary to produce speech. The bellows serve as an analogue to the lungs. ... Attached to the bellows there is a small wooden box called the windchest. In this there is a vibrating reed pipe functioning as an analog to the glottis. The reed pipe leads into the vocal tract which itself leads into a rubber funnel which represents the oral cavity. (Brackhane 2017 C)

Although Kempelen left out important articulators such as teeth and alveolar ridge, he did conceptualize two "independent articulatory movements," which in the design of his Mechanism were separated into the mouth opening and "the 'tongue channel'" (Brackhane 2015: 47) as well as a mechanism for "mimicking nasal sounds" such as m and n (Lindsay 1997: 58). He honed the sound quality of his machine in at least two major overhauls, suggesting finally that a simple keyboard be added to facilitate real-time voice synthesis (Dudley and Tanroczy 1950: 163). Kempelen's empirical approach and resulting theories of vocalization, unlike Kratzenstein's, still align with contemporary speech research. Although he never reached his ultimate aim to produce all human speech sounds, he is sometimes considered "the founder of experimental phonetics" (Brackhane 2015: 48). His original speaking machine likely does not exist, but a replica constructed around 1800 following Kempelen's design was shown at the Deutsches Museum in Munich.

In 1815, German scholar Joseph Faber, inspired by Kempelen's book, set out to improve upon the design (Talking Machine 1880). By 1841, he began exhibiting his device—contracting with P.T. Barnum to show the talking machine at London's Egyptian Hall (Story 2019: 10). This machine had a vibrating rubber larynx along with a hinged jaw, ivory tongue, and "nose" valve controlled by an articulatory keyboard, as well as cheeks made of rubber (Talking Machine 1880; Lindsay 1997; Story 2019). A component resembling a windmill produced "the rattle of the letter 'r'" (Talking Machine 1880). Faber's machine was described as superior to English scientist Charles Wheatstone's speaking device since it could utter entire sentences instead of words and phrases (Story 2019).

Unfortunately for Faber, by the early nineteenth century, acoustic theorists were leaving behind models of physical production like Kempelen's, which simulated speech with mechanical replicas of the vocal apparatus, and instead focusing on voice frequencies themselves. In response to Faber's talking machine, British researcher Robert Willis built a system of expandable tubes and reeds around 1830 which synthesized vocal sound without replicating vocal physiology (Story 2019). This alternative approach, which investigated the spectral (or frequency) components of sound rather than its production, became an important scientific direction over the following century. The success of inventions such as Thomas Edison's phonograph and Alexander Graham Bell's telephone in the 1870s consigned Faber's speaking machine to historical obscurity (Lindsay 1997).

1.3.2 *Helmholtz and Simple Tones*

Hermann von Helmholtz (1821–1894) was trained as a physician and expounded his knowledge of physiology in two manuals describing vision and hearing in the 1840s and 1850s, books that remain foundational even today. In the following decades, he delved into electrodynamics and thermodynamics, and even the philosophy of science, earning the apt moniker of polymath (Schmidgen 2018). Helmholtz strove to explain physical phenomena in terms of mechanics, applying mathematics developed in the previous century to (among many other problems) describe the periodic vibration of a taut string (Heidelberger 2006). Rather than understanding the characteristic sound of the human voice by building an instrument modeled after the vocal mechanism in order to create speechlike tones, Helmholtz tested the longstanding theory that every sound is composed of what he called simple tones: periodic waveforms that have no harmonic components, just one measurable frequency of vibration—what we now call sinusoidal or sine waves. Helmholtz's expression of all sounds as their harmonic (or spectral) content also proved at least as productive and influential as Kempelen's physical model from a century earlier. Thus, complex sounds like those produced by musical instruments or the human voice could be understood by analyzing their harmonics—the overtone frequencies that give these sounds their rich timbre.

The mathematics that enabled this approach was developed by mathematicians such as Daniel Bernoulli (1700–1782), Leonard Euler (1707–1783), Jean de Rond d'Alembert (1717–1783), and most famously Jean-Baptiste Joseph Fourier (1768–1830). Helmholtz built upon equations and propositions with practical experiments in physiological acoustics. In 1857, he attempted to determine the harmonic content of vowels, building an apparatus consisting of a set of tuning forks, "each of which is supplied with a corresponding resonator and tuned to produce a harmonic series of pure tones" (Vogel 1994: 274). This control over individual frequencies allowed Helmholtz to create more complex waveforms, with the sounds emitted by this apparatus resembling sung vowels (Vogel 1994). In this sense, Helmholtz was able to acoustically synthesize specific, harmonically complex timbres from a combination of simple sonic components—the 'pure' sinusoidal vibrations of the tuning forks set to different frequencies. Helmholtz's work was a precursor to later advancements in acoustics and sound synthesis, contributing to the understanding of how complex, natural sounds like vowels could be analyzed (broken down) into and synthesized (built) from mathematically simpler sine waves.

Helmholtz also designed a set of devices, now known as Helmholtz resonators, that enabled him to isolate and identify the specific frequencies present in any complex sound. This work supported the idea that any timbre could be broken down into a finite set of acoustically pure waveforms. These pure waveforms, called sine waves (or sinusoidal waves), are mathematically simple and characterized by a smooth periodic oscillation with equal rises and falls. While perfect sine waves are rare in natural sounds, they now form the foundation for analyzing more complex sound waves. In the twentieth century, techniques such as spectral analysis emerged, allowing scientists and audio engineers to break down sound waves into their component frequencies. This approach has become crucial in both the study and creation of new sounds, as it provides a deeper understanding of how different frequencies combine to produce the unique timbres we hear.

In *On the Sensations of Tone as a Physiological Basis for the Theory of Music*, Helmholtz describes his resonators and their use as "hollow spheres of glass or metal, or tubes, with two openings. ... One opening (a) has sharp edges, the other (b) is funnel-shaped, and adapted for insertion into the ear" (Helmholtz 1877/1954: 43). Understood in contemporary terms, the prime tone (or fundamental F0) is produced by sympathetic vibration of the air inside the resonator, with the frequency of the tone derivable in mathematical relation to the volume of the sphere. A properly tuned set of resonators of different sizes could be used to identify the overtones (upper harmonics) of any sound (Helmholtz 1877/1954). Furthermore, Helmholtz asserted that humans perceive sound in the same way: "[T]he human ear really does analyse musical tones according to the law of simple vibrations" (Helmholtz 1877/1954: 52). He provided physiological description of the parts of the ear that not only showed how the eardrum and small bones of the ear vibrate sympathetically with sound waves in the air, but also how "the sonorous vibrations of the air in the outer auditory passage are finally transferred to the membranes of the labyrinth, more especially those of the cochlea, and to the expansions of the nerves upon them" (Helmholtz 1877/1954: 138). While his understanding of how the nerves functioned was limited, Helmholtz logically deduced that "every tone of determinate pitch will be felt only by certain nerve fibres, and simple tones of different pitch will excite different fibres" (147–148)—a deduction now widely accepted as empirical fact (Shepard 1999; Pierce 1999; Cheveigné 2010).

1.4 How Do We Hear a Voice?

1.4.1 Defining Voice: A Moving Target

Helmholtz and his empirical research into the nature of sound and auditory perception indicated the materiality and measurability of both. Sound waves are captured and funneled by the pinna (or auricle), the visible part of the ear, into the ear canal toward the middle ear. The resulting vibration of the eardrum and ossicles (small bones in the middle ear) is transmitted to the cochlea, a coiled structure in the inner ear containing ligaments, fluid, and membranes, including the basilar membrane, which is lined with hair cells. These hair cells, part of the cochlea's organ of Corti, convert the mechanical vibrations of sound into electrical signals, which then travel along the auditory nerve to the brain. The arrangement of hair cells along the basilar membrane of the cochlea is organized according to frequency sensitivity, with the lowest frequencies being processed by hair cells in the outer part of the cochlea and higher frequencies in the inner part (Mathews 1999). Contemporary research has built upon Helmholtz's work; current findings suggest that the perception of pitch may be more dependent on temporal patterns of neural firing within the auditory nervous system, rather than being determined solely by the location of maximal vibration along the cochlea as proposed by Helmholtz in his place theory of pitch perception (De Boer and Nuttall 2010: 95). Yet Helmholtz's legacy remains so great, his conjectures upon the function of the ear persist (Cheveigné 2010).

This general and generalizable conception of sound then connects both sides of the human equation; the production and the perception of voice are inextricably linked. As Frühholz and Belin observe, "[A]ny attempt at a definition [of voice] needs to deal with the fact that every voice has usually two sides to its existence, which makes that definition of a voice a juggling between perspectives. The two sides are the production of a voice on one side, and the perception of a voice on the other side" (2018: 5). Thus, we can further elaborate our working definition: voice is sound created by a human's vibrating vocal folds, resonated by the cavities of head and throat and shaped by the articulatory system to form vowels and consonants; this sound is then perceived by a listener as having been produced by a human body in this way.

For when we consider the perceptual side, we must then deal with the fact that vocal sound can be produced by someone that may remain forever unseen by a listener. Conversely, once a human sound is uttered, that vocalization is immediately outside the body of its origin, traveling to listeners beyond the scope and control of the speaker. Today, we live surrounded by technologies that transmit and reproduce not only voices of those far away or no longer living, but even voices of entities lacking any human origin whatsoever. As illustrated by the case of my listening experience of kyaami's "Mahō" cover using the Yuzuki Yukari Vocaloid voicebank, the question of how a listener decides whether a sound is a 'human voice' is increasingly complicated.

1.4.2 Knowing the World Through Sound

The sound of a voice is sensed not inside the listener's ear alone. Eidsheim (2018) suggests that "the voice does not arise solely from the vocalizer; it is created just as much within the process of listening" (Eidsheim 2018: 11). Our ears, brains, voices, and bodies evolved in the creation of individual functional organisms that exist in natural environments and social contexts. This means that hearing interacts with the other senses as well as our memory sense of time. Belin (2019) posits that listeners extract key information from the sound of a voice, including the physical and personality traits of the person vocalizing. We listen for both stable and transient physical characteristics. Constructing an auditory face based on voice cues such as vocal tone, pitch, and emotional expression allows us both to recognize a speaker in future interactions and to predict how those interactions might unfold (Belin 2019: 37–38).

Certain functions of perception even seem to be hardwired into our auditory systems. For example, studies indicate that listeners across cultures associate a low voice with a large body size (of either sex), despite there being minimal empirical evidence connecting body size with vocal pitch (within sex categories). Pisanski and Bryant (2019) note that such an unconscious perceptual bias goes beyond biological characteristics, as "some researchers have suggested that the perceived association between low voice frequencies and large body size represents a deep-rooted and very general perceptual bias linking any low-frequency sound to largeness" (Pisanski and Bryant 2019: 274).

The listener takes in a stream of vibratory information in the form of soundwaves and the auditory system, which includes the brain, makes sense of the patterns of this input in conjunction with other sensory information. One example of how this works is termed loudness constancy. In the case of the human visual system, we understand that, although objects seem smaller as they move farther from our eye, they remain the same size—a phenomenon called size constancy (Shepard 1999: 25). Likewise for the human auditory system, if a sounding object or instrument making a constant sound moves away from a listener, the intensity of that sound (experienced as loudness) decreases from the listener's perspective—even if the intensity remains objectively the same (Shepard 1999: 25). Just like the visual object that appears smaller the farther away it gets, a sound seems quieter the further it gets from a listener.

Perceptual completion is another key phenomenon in human perception. Because our senses can only process a limited amount of information at any given time, our perceptual systems must integrate both bottom-up and top-down processing to make sense of the sensory data. This means that humans unconsciously fill in information "to determine the most probable explanation for what is occurring in the real world that is consistent with the information presented to our senses" (Shepard 1999: 29–30). In short, our perceptual systems, as part of the brain's overall function, are highly adaptable to changes in the real world, enabling us to function effectively in accordance with its laws. One main appeal of technology is that it promises us the power to change our relationship with the world. But how far can this promise truly take us?

References

Ayukawa, Pate. 2022. *Tōkyō Daigaku Bōkaroido Ongakuron Kōgi*. [University of Tokyo's Vocaloid Music Theory Lectures] Tokyo: Bungei Shunjū.

Belin, Pascal. 2019. The 'Vocal Brain': Core and Extended Cerebral Networks for Voice Processing. In *The Oxford Handbook of Voice Studies*, ed. Nina Sun Eidsheim and Katherine Meizel, 37–60. Oxford: Oxford University Press.

Brackhane, Fabian. 2015. Kempelen vs. Kratzenstein—Researchers on Speech Synthesis in Times of Change. *First International Workshop on the History of Speech Communication Research, Dresden, Germany* 4–5 September. Accessed 19 November 2024. http://www.isca-speech.org/archive

Brackhane, Fabian. 2017. Preface. In *The Mechanism of Human Speech by Wolfgang von Kempelen*, ed. Fabian Brackhane, Richard Sproat, and Jürgen Trouvain, XCI–CL. Dresden: TUD Press.

Cheveigné, Alain. 2010. Pitch Perception. In *Oxford Handbook of Auditory Science: Hearing*, ed. Christopher Plack, 71–104. Oxford: Oxford University Press. https://doi.org/10.1093/oxfordhb/9780199233557.013.0004.

Condry, Ian. 2011. Miku: Japan's Virtual Idol and Media Platform. *Civic Media: Creating Technology for Social Change*. Website. https://civic.mit.edu/index.html%3Fp=1749.html

Cook, Perry R. 1999a. Formant Peaks and Spectral Valleys. In *Music, Cognition and Computerized Sound: An Introduction to Psychoacoustics*, ed. Perry R. Cook, 139–147. Cambridge: MIT Press.

Cook, Perry R. 1999b. Pitch, Periodicity, and Noise in the Voice. In *Music, Cognition and Computerized Sound: An Introduction to Psychoacoustics*, ed. Perry R. Cook, 195–208. Cambridge: MIT Press.

Dayme, Meribeth Bunch. 2005. *The Performer's Voice: Realizing Your Vocal Potential*. New York: Norton.

De Boer, Egbert, and Alfred Nuttall. 2010. Cochlear Mechanics, Tuning, Non-Linearities. In *Oxford Handbook of Auditory Science: The Ear*, ed. Paul Fuchs, 139–178. Oxford: Oxford University Press. https://doi.org/10.1093/oxfordhb/9780199233397.013.0005.

Dudley, Homer, and T. H. Tarnoczy. 1950. The Speaking Machine of Wolfgang von Kempelen. *Journal of the Acoustical Society of America* 22:151–166.

Eidsheim, Nina Sun. 2018. *The Race of Sound: Listening, Timbre and Vocality in African American Music*. Durham: Duke University Press.

Frühholz, Sascha, and Pascal Belin. 2018. The Science of Voice Perception. In *The Oxford Handbook of Voice Perception*, ed. Sascha Frühholz and Pascal Belin, 3–14. Oxford: Oxford University Press. https://doi.org/10.1093/oxfordhb/9780198743187.013.1.

Fullkawa Honpo. 2012. *Girlfriend from Kyoto*. Compact Disc. Tokyo: Space Shower Networks, PECF-3031.

Hamasaki, Masahiro, Hideaki Takeda, Tom Hope, and Takuichi Nishimura. 2009. Network Analysis of an Emergent Massively Collaborative Creation Community: How Can People Create Videos Collaboratively without Collaboration? *Proceedings of the International AAAI Conference on Web and Social Media* 3(1): 222–225. Accessed 14 October 2014. https://doi.org/10.1609/icwsm.v3i1.14000

Hatsune Miku no Shōshitsu Honki de Utatte Mita [I Tried My Best to Sing "End of Hatsune Miku"]. 2021. *nory*. YouTube. https://www.youtube.com/watch?v=46IdeeI3Smg

Heidelberger, Michael. 2006. Helmholtz, Hermann von. In *Europe 1789–1914: Encyclopedia of the Age of Industry and Empire, Vol. 2*, ed. John Merriman and Jay Winter, 1057–1059. Detroit: Charles Scribner's Sons.

Helmholtz, Hermann von. 1877/1954. *On the Sensations of Tone as a Physiological Basis for the Theory of Music*. Translated by Alexander J. Ellis. New York: Dover Publications.

Jiang, Jack. 2015. Physiology of Voice Production: How Does the Voice Work? In *The Performer's Voice*, ed. Michael S. Benninger, Thomas Murry, and Michael M. Johns, vol. III, 39–52. San Diego: Plural Publishing.

Kempelen, Wolfgang von. 1791/2017. *The Mechanism of Human Speech Along with the Description of His Speaking Machine*. Translated by Richard Sproat. Dresden: TUD Press.

Kitamura, Yasuyuki. 2014. Miku to Kyōen Shitemita: Lady Gaga [Lady Gaga: I Performed with Miku]. In *Poketto Miku Kōshiki Bukku*, 22–23. Tokyo: Gakken Educational Publishing.

Lindsay, David. 1997. Talking Head. *Invention and Technology: The Magazine of Innovation* 1:56–63.

Maragos, Nicolas. 2015. Anatomy of the Vocal Mechanism: Structure of the Voice. In *The Performer's Voice*, ed. Michael S. Benninger, Thomas Murry, and Michael M. Johns, vol. III, 31–38. San Diego: Plural Publishing.

Mathews, Max. 1999. The Ear and How It Works. In *Music, Cognition and Computerized Sound: An Introduction to Psychoacoustics*, ed. Perry R. Cook, 1–10. Cambridge: MIT Press.

Ningen ga Utaenai Kyoku wo Utattemitara Katsuzetsu ga Shinda wwww "Hatsune Miku no Gekishō" [I Tried Singing the Song No Human Can Sing and My Tongue Died LOL "Intense Voice of Hatsune Miku"]. 2021. *Ganmendoshakuzure.* YouTube. https://www.youtube.com/watch?v=aiMLsp5AdyU

[Official] THE END OF HATSUNE MIKU / cosMo@Bousou-P. 2018. *cosMo@bousouP Official Channel.* YouTube. https://www.youtube.com/watch?v=VWVtIg5cdDU

[Official] The Intense Voice of HATSUNE MIKU / cosMo@Bousou-P. 2018. *cosMo@bousouP Official Channel.* YouTube. https://www.youtube.com/watch?v=MFEaIgMkR_0

Olive, Joseph P. 1998. "The Talking Computer": Text to Speech Synthesis. In *HAL's Legacy: 2001's Computer as Dream and Reality*, ed. David G. Stork, 101–129. Cambridge, MA: MIT Press.

Pierce, John. 1999. Hearing in Space and Time. In *Music, Cognition and Computerized Sound: An Introduction to Psychoacoustics*, ed. Perry R. Cook, 89–103. Cambridge: MIT Press.

Pisanski, Katarzyna, and Gregory Bryant. 2019. The Evolution of Voice Perception. In *The Oxford Handbook of Voice Studies*, ed. Nina Sun Eidsheim and Katherine Meizel, 269–300. Oxford: Oxford University Press. https://doi.org/10.1093/oxfordhb/9780199982295.013.36.

Scherer, Klaus. 2019. Acoustic Patterning of Emotion Vocalizations. In *The Oxford Handbook of Voice Perception*, ed. Sascha Frühholz and Pascal Belin, 61–92. Oxford: Oxford University Press.

Schmidgen, Henning. 2018. The Last Polymath. *Nature* 561:175.

Shepard, Roger. 1999. Cognitive Psychology and Music. In *Music, Cognition and Computerized Sound: An Introduction to Psychoacoustics*, ed. Perry R. Cook, 21–35. Cambridge: MIT Press.

Story, Brad. 2019. History of Speech Synthesis. In *Routledge Handbook of Phonetics*, ed. William Katz and Peter Assmann, 9–33. London: Routledge.

Suetsugu, Satoshi. 2013. Bōkaroido Kakō: Gendai ni Okeru Uta no Hassei wo Megutte. [A Study of Vocaloid Singing: On the Contemporary Production of Song]. *Kyoto Seika Daigaku Kiyō* 43 (2): 48–63.

Sundberg, Johan. 2019. The Singing Voice. In *The Oxford Handbook of Voice Perception*, ed. Sascha Frühholz and Pascal Belin, 117–142. Oxford: Oxford University Press.

Takahashi Nobuyuki/Studio Hard Deluxe. 2011. *Bōkaroido Genshō: Shinseiki Kontentsu Sangyō no Mirai Moderu* [Vocaloid Phenomenon: A Future Model for the Content Industry in the New Century]. Tokyo: PHP Institute.

Talking Machine. 1880. *Journal of the Society for Arts* 28 (1435): 609.

The Disappearance of Hatsune Miku (THE END OF HATSUNE MIKU)/cover. 2023. *NIJIRO ZAMURAI*. YouTube. https://www.youtube.com/watch?v=Ko6AGlyDeqY

Titze, Ingo. 2008. The Human Instrument. *Scientific American Magazine* 298:1. https://www.scientificamerican.com/article/the-human-instrument/.

Vogel, Stephan. 1994. Sensation of Tone, Perception of Sound, and Empiricism. In *Hermann von Helmholtz and the Foundations of Nineteenth-century Science*, ed. David Cahan, 259–287. Berkeley: University of California Press.

Yang, Jeff. 2011. In the World of Auto-Tune, Can a Computer Create a Star? *Wall Street Journal*. Accessed 5 October 2024. https://www.wsj.com/articles/BL-SEB-67903

Yuzuki Yukari Mahou Mahō Kabā. [Yuzuki Yukari Cover of "Mahou" Magic]. 2014. *kyaami*. YouTube. Uploaded 30 March 2014. Accessed 4 April 2016. https://www.youtube.com/watch?v=01uN4MCsrCE

CHAPTER 2

Out of the Analog Age: Singing Robots and the Uncanny Valley

Abstract This chapter opens with a case study of a 1979 Japanese song featuring vocoder, illustrating how robotic singing voices have been perceived and aestheticized. It also briefly highlights creative pioneers like Wendy Carlos, who worked with vocoders, and introduces similar vocal effects such as the Sonovox. The chapter examines the historical significance of Homer Dudley's groundbreaking inventions—the vocoder and the voder—as an innovation in signal processing and a commercially nonviable product, respectively. Dudley's approach to signal processing was built upon Helmholtz' perceptual theories, laying the groundwork for spectral analysis. The chapter also introduces the inception of the source-filter model of speech, a theoretical model that proposes vocalization is generated by the vocal cords (the source) and then modified by the vocal tract (the filter). This process was often modeled using electrical circuits, which contributed to the development of spectral analysis methods for speech. The influence on singing synthesis of 1952 Gunnar Fant's OVE formant synthesizer is traced through the development of Music and Singing Synthesis Equipment (MUSSE). Fales' account of the role of formants in aural perception is discussed, followed by an overview of Mori's influential concept of the uncanny valley and its applications in both audio and audiovisual media. The chapter concludes with two contrasting case studies of film music, illustrating how context and expectation influence uncanny valley effects in mediated experiences. One case examines how

© The Author(s), under exclusive license to Springer Nature Switzerland AG 2025
G. Jude, *How Vocaloid Works*,
https://doi.org/10.1007/978-3-031-92727-0_2

altering formants using Vocaloid enhanced uncanny valley-type effects in an animated film by Satoshi Kon, while the other looks at how the unremarkably human-sounding voice of HAL9000 in *2001: A Space Odyssey* was made eerily unsettling.

Keywords Musical vocoder • YMO's "Behind the Mask" (1979) • Source-filter model applications • Music and Singing Synthesis Equipment (MUSSE) • Perceptualization • Vocal uncanny valley • *Paprika* (2006) • Susumu Hirasawa's Vocaloid songs • HAL9000's voice

2.1 Solid State Vocoder: Yellow Magic Orchestra's "Behind the Mask," 1979

Decades before the rise of Hatsune Miku and her clan of virtual pop idols, another electronic singing technology emerged from Japan, one which sounded purposely inhuman. Technopop band Yellow Magic Orchestra (YMO) were not the first musicians to use a vocoder in their music, but the Japanese band's influence brought the vocoder's robotic sound into global popular music history. Formed in 1978, the groundbreaking Japanese trio of Haruomi Hosono, Yukihiro Takahashi, and Ryuichi Sakamoto (with collaborators Hideki Matsutake and Akiko Yano) famously used the vocoder, an early twentieth-century voice encoding hardware, to create evocative vocal effects. Inspired by innovators such as West Germany's Kraftwerk, YMO established an appealing yet subversive sonic style with cutting-edge electronics, influencing early 1980s hip-hop artists like Afrika Bambaataa and inaugurating an aesthetic that associated cybernetic aural (and visual) imagery with an appealing futuristic positionality for outsiders and rebels (Jude 2018).

In one of their biggest international hits, "Behind the Mask," from their 1979 sophomore album *Solid State Survivor*, the robotic quality of Ryuichi Sakamoto's vocoder-effected singing evokes a posthuman symbiosis of (Japanese) human and machine (Yellow Magic Orchestra 1979). Sakamoto's robotized melody line, delivering English lyrics written by Chris Modell barely intelligible through the vocoder's distortion, sounds half buried in electronic circuitry. The keyboard input[1] that controls the

---

[1] Sakamoto used the Roland VP-330 vocoder on *Solid State Survivor*, after using the Korg VC-10 vocoder on his debut solo album, *Thousand Knives*, and the band's first release, *Yellow Magic Orchestra*, both in 1978 (Fujii 2019).

vocoder pitch multiplies Sakamoto's voice into harmony with itself. Concert footage from their 1979 global tour highlights the processed musical style through the use of the era's cutting-edge video effects (Yellow Magic Orchestra 2000).

As the band's name suggests, Yellow Magic Orchestra playfully challenged racial stereotypes and national hierarchies, exemplified in "Behind the Mask" through its contrast of a dehumanized vocal timbre and provocative lyrics with an upbeat pop tune. In their performance of self-consciously Japanese identity that pushed the boundaries of human identity, YMO created a unique sound that pushed past the binary notion that Japanese music was either 'traditional' or 'imitative' of imported Western genres. Within Japan, the band's troubling of the boundary between imitation and authenticity was a high stakes move for a culture emerging out from under decades of post-war American political and cultural dominance (Jude 2018).

Yet YMO's appeal crossed racial, national, and cultural boundaries. "Behind the Mask" was so appealing that it was covered by English rock icon Eric Clapton; Michael Jackson revised the lyrics with the intention of releasing his own version of the song on his *Thriller* album in 1982—although copyright battles delayed the track's release until 2010 (Fujii 2019; Balmont 2023). The robotic vocal sound has remained a staple in numerous genres of popular music, paving the way for both audience reception and artists' integration of synthesized vocal timbres—including the early uses of Vocaloid.

2.2 Robot Voice, from Code to Music

2.2.1 Bell Telephone Laboratories, 1922–1945

In 1922, John Q. Stewart, an American physicist, published his research on the electrical generation of artificial vowels, which he had completed while working at American Telephone and Telegraph Company (AT&T) (Stewart 1972). Stewart simulated acoustic resonances of the vocal mechanism by varying the oscillations of an analog circuit, using control knobs to quickly shift resonance frequencies (Story 2019). As Stewart (who spent most of his life as an astrophysicist) noted, the real challenge was "manipulation of the apparatus to imitate the manifold variations in tone which are so important in securing naturalness" (Stewart qtd. in Story

2019: 14). Later in the twentieth century, Stewart's method of electronic voice synthesis was elaborated into a form of voice synthesis called formant synthesis (Story 2019).

In 1927, Homer Dudley, a research engineer at AT&T's newly established Bell Telephone Laboratories, began working on a means of compressing speech for more efficient telephone transmission across long distances (Mills 2012; Story 2019). Within a decade, Dudley had patented his system of speech encoding, which he called "signal transmission" (Dudley 1939a)—also known as the vocoder (voice encoder) (Dudley 1939b). The vocoder uses electronic filters to separate vocal input (the modulating signal) into component frequency bands, or channels (Dudley 1940). These filters function similarly to Helmholtz's acoustic resonators, isolating the frequencies of the sound. Then the amplitude of each frequency band is encoded for transmission.

The vocoder receiving the encoded transmission automatically synthesizes the simplified version of the shifting spectral (or frequency spectrum) waveform into a nonhuman but intelligible speech sound. The pitch of the voice is resynthesized by substituting the electrical buzz of an oscillator (a circuit emitting a periodic signal, such as a sine wave), which results in the synthesized output remaining monotone. However, the frequency ranges that distinguish vowels from each other, as well as the noise and disruptions of consonants, are preserved as the most basic components required to convey the meaning of the message (Dudley 1939a, b, 1940). This extraction of speech features facilitated the effective and efficient transmission of information across longer distances.

The vocoder became an important component of the Allies' WWII-era secure communications encryption system, SIGSALY. Its success paved the way for digital speech compression and encryption technologies, such as LPC (linear predictive coding), which are still used in today's cell phone networks. Other vocoding techniques have also been developed, with Dudley's original innovation later being designated as the channel vocoder, due to its use of multiple frequency channels—originally ten, with the frequency ranges selected by ear (Mills 2012).

2.2.2 *Homer Dudley's Voder, 1939*

Dudley's voder (voice operation demonstrator) went a step further than the vocoder, allowing a human operator to artificially produce intelligible electronic 'speech' in real time using manual keyboard controls rather than vocal input (Dudley 1938). The voder's 'larynx' was a buzzy electronic oscillator that produced the fundamental frequency, while the resonance of its 'vocal tract' was achieved through selection of appropriate filters; an electrical noise generator produced the hiss of unvoiced speech articulation (Smith 2010). First demonstrated at the 1939 New York World's Fair, speech synthesis using the voder was a performance skill which required a year of rigorous training for its Voderettes—so named because the two dozen virtuosic operators were all female—to master (Mills 2012). The system controls were complex: an organ-like keyboard and foot pedal to control F0 pitch and inflection, with a wrist bar to switch between buzz (for voiced sounds) or hiss (for unvoiced sounds) (Bell 2024); the keyboard also selected from the ten filter bands to simulate articulation of vowel resonance (Dudley 1938). These complex manipulations of electrical circuitry produced intelligible, if clearly artificial, utterances.

In a sense, the voder was the fulfillment of Kempelen's dream of a voice synthesizer that utilized Helmholtz's spectral approach. Yet despite its dramatic premier—demonstrating the "World of Tomorrow" at AT&T's pavilion daily for eighteen months (Bell 2024)—the voder did not gain wide popularity for vocal synthesis. As Bell points out, the device was not marketable to the public, being far too difficult to operate and lacking practical application in daily life (Bell 2024). It did, however, play a significant role in introducing the notion that machines could speak—and even sing (Bell 2024).

2.2.3 Dudley's Musical Legacy Since 1948

Dudley himself recognized the musical potential of his inventions, stating that the vocoder had "extraordinary possibilities to produce music of sorts never heard before" (Dudley 1938: 4). In 1948, Dudley delivered a vocoder to Dr. Werner Meyer-Eppler, a speech researcher at Bonn University (Manning 2013). Other West German researchers and musicians were fascinated by Dr. Meyer-Eppler's presentations on his work with the device, and by 1956, composers and engineers at the Siemens Studio für Elektronische Musik in Munich had developed a vocoder specifically for musical uses (Manning 2013). In the early 1960s, music engineer Robert Moog invented more affordable modular synthesizer components that made previously expensive analog sound-making equipment more widely accessible (Holmes 2020). Electronic musician Wendy Carlos used her Moog equipment to encode and decode vocals, with collaborator Rachel Elkind's 'articulations' as input, effectively patching together an ad-hoc vocoder (Rachel Elkind-Tourre 2000). Carlos' vocoder reworkings of Beethoven were famously featured in Kubrick's 1971 dystopic film *A Clockwork Orange*. By the late 1970s, instruments such as Moog's 16-channel vocoder made the robotic voice part of many musicians' sound-making repertoires.

Other machine-like vocal effects produce similar sounds to the vocoder, distorting the voice and adding a metallic or automated quality. The Sonovox,[2] invented in the 1930s, replaces the glottal wave with an electronically produced input; a small transducer is placed on the throat and shaped by a vocalist's own vocal tract, creating an effect where a recorded sound seems to be 'sung' or 'spoken.' The talk-box aims an instrumental input through a tube into the mouth to be articulated. This vocal effect has been popularized by artists in the 1970s, 1980s, and 1990s, from Stevie Wonder to Zapp's Roger Troutman to Daft Punk.

Just like the vocoder, these instruments replace the fundamental frequency coming from the larynx. However, the Sonovox and the talk-box, which use the mouth as an acoustic filter, differ significantly from the voder and vocoder. With the Sonovox and talk-box, the formant frequencies resonated through the mouth and upper throat shape the sound, functioning more like a jaw harp. In contrast, the voder and vocoder are entirely electronically synthesized. Regardless of design or function, the appeal of such 'unnatural' vocal effects remains audible in the digital distortion of overdriven Auto-Tune pitch correction software repurposed by artists such as Cher in the late 1990s and T-Pain in the 2000s (Duinker 2025). Audiences and artists have not only grown accustomed to such robotic sounds—we have enthusiastically embraced the aesthetic potential of a range of obviously synthesized vocals. To understand the limits of this appeal, as well as how humans sense the distinction between organic human utterances and synthesized ones, we must delve deeper into the central role of formants in human vocalization and perception.

---

[2] Famously demonstrated by young actress Lucile Ball on CBS in 1939. https://www.britishpathe.com/asset/68426/

2.3 Formant Frequencies: Functions and Effects

2.3.1 The Source-Filter Model

In 1941, Japanese phoneticists Tsutomu Chiba and Masato Kajiyama proposed a theory of speech production based on representing the human vocal tract as one (or more) cylindrical tubes, similar to Kempelen's mechanical model (Smith 2010: 451). Chiba and Kajiyama's computational approach to the physical voice modeling incorporated modern tools such as electrical circuitry and X-ray imaging that measured vocal tract shapes (Arai 2004: C-116), allowing the calculation of the voice's frequency spectra—a model that Smith (2010) refers to as a "vocal tract analog model" (Smith 2010: 451). This groundbreaking work of Chiba and Kajiyama laid the foundation for understanding the relationship between physical articulation and the spectral characteristics of speech sounds, influencing the development of the source-filter model of vocal production by Swedish speech scientist Gunnar Fant (Fant 1960, 2001; Arai 2004).

The source-filter model treats the vocal tract as a set of filters, whereby some frequencies or wavelengths of sound produced by the glottis are attenuated and some are amplified. This filtering effect results in the formation of formants, the distinctive peaks in frequency range that characterize human articulation. This is crucial in understanding the human production and perception of vowel sounds (Fant 1960, 2004). According to source-filter theory, different vowels are associated with different formants, which can be recognized despite variations in speakers' vocal tracts (e.g., length, size, or thickness of vocal folds). Phonetic theory classifies vowels according to the position of the tongue in the mouth: front, central, or back, and in a range between high and low positions; each of these tongue positions results in audibly distinct vowel sounds (Pickett 1999).

The source-filter model also shows that the voice's fundamental frequency (F0) (which determines the voice's pitch) and formant frequencies (which determine vowel articulation) are "largely independent of one another" (Pisanski and Bryant 2019: 274). Chiba and Kajiyama postulated that formants occur in "a fixed ratio rather than absolute values" (Arai C-117). This means that, due to human physiology, a person can shape their mouth to achieve these formant frequency bands and be understood no matter what the size of their own mouth. What is remarkable about this model is that it allows us to understand how humans can distinguish one another's mouth shapes and movements based on the frequency content produced by those shapes and movements. In other words, by combining the insights of physical models (how the vocal apparatus works) and spectral models (how sounds are constituted and perceived), formant theory explains how each vowel is defined by characteristic frequency bands, independent of the fundamental pitch. In other words, the physical model of vocal production and the spectral model of voice perception can be understood as complementary. Moreover, since formant peaks in the resonant frequencies of the vocal tract can be mathematically defined, they can be electronically synthesized, contributing to voice synthesis technologies.

2.3.2 OVE and MUSSE

The source-filter model ultimately led to one of the earliest attempts to electronically synthesize musical vocalization rather than speech. Gunnar Fant's 1953 electronic vowel synthesizer, the Orator Verbis Electris (OVE), was an example of a category of speech synthesis the later became known as formant synthesis (Story 2019). OVE in turn inspired Fant's fellow researchers at Stockholm's KTH Royal Institute of Technology to invent Music and Singing Synthesis Equipment, or MUSSE (Sundberg 1978, 2007; Chan 2020). MUSSE connected hardware analog components, namely controllers (including a keyboard, dials, switches, and a joystick) and oscillators, later incorporating a computer that calculated the formant amplitudes and bandwidths (Sundberg 1978, 2007; Chan 2020). The distinction between OVE and MUSSE was the salient difference between spoken and musical utterances: "formant frequencies and other synthesis variables should be continuously variable rather than variable in small but discrete steps" (Sundberg 2007: 9). That is, the synthesized sounds should allow for longer, song-like vocalization. As Sundberg wrote in 1978, MUSSE allowed further exploration of "what it is that makes singing sound like singing" (Sundberg 1978: 111).

The source-filter model and the idea of vocal formants begin to account for the complexity of the changing patterns that make up what we perceive when we hear a human voice. Part of what makes a channel vocoder sound robotic is not just the lack of a human's expressively varying fundamental frequency (which provides melody in song and intonation in speech), but also the absence of the crucial formant frequency peaks. Vocoders' fixed frequency ranges of filter banks fail to capture the organic variability and nuances of formants. Formant ratios, which are patterned in specific ways, are key to characterizing the distinctive qualities of the human voice. These ratios reflect the internal resonances of a sounding, embodied voice, and understanding them is crucial for the development of synthesized singing and speech that approximates human vocal qualities. But how do we hear these particular frequency patterns as characteristically human?

2.3.3 Formants: How Hearing Makes a Sound(ing Body)

Cornelia Fales explores the significance of formants through a concept she terms *perceptualization* (Fales 2002). This refers to "any cognitive operation or feature that contributes to the perceptual outcome of a signal beyond the actual acoustic elements of the signal" (Fales 2002: 63). Perceptualization suggests that what we hear is not identical to what is objectively measurable. For instance, this difference is evident when comparing pitch perception to frequency (see Chap. 1). Fales further explains that auditory perception is inherently source-oriented and rule-based, enabling us to efficiently process the complex, dynamic stream of vibratory input in order to react appropriately to important phenomena in our surroundings (Fales 2005). In other words, survival depends on our ability to know *That's a tiger growling in the bush* and quickly *Run away!*

The perceived sonic world results from the interactive yet preconscious relationship between the acoustic input of a listener's surroundings and the listener's internal processes. We actively select acoustic vibrations from our environment, guided by a cognitive propensity to identify them as indicating a particular source or ontological origin. The concept of perceptualization describes how a listener identifies and combines "necessary interpretive elements" from the acoustic properties of the environment to create auditory perceptions (Fales 2002: 63). As a source-oriented process, auditory perception also relies on prior knowledge and expectations based on context. Fales (2005) further considers perceptualization in terms of how human hearing operates through *perceptual fusion*.

Perceptual fusion refers to how the auditory system processes simultaneous acoustic elements into a unified sense of a sound source or percept (Fales 2005). The system analyzes an object of perception by using "the same source characteristics that it has used to construct the percept to begin with" (Fales 2005: 163). This self-reinforcing process highlights the fallibility of aural perception: our belief that what we hear correlates with a known and predictable world is built upon our confidence in that correlation (Fales 2005). We are, by necessity, primed to believe our ears.

Additionally, the degree of perceptualization required for auditory processing of formant resonances is comparatively greater than for auditory processing of harmonic ones: "The difference between harmonically-structured and formant-based timbres centers on the unit of perceptual salience—that is, on whether single harmonics or entire formants dictate timbral quality" (Fales 2002: 72). Since formants are, by definition, resonance patterns of the human vocal tract, hearing 'voice' formants involves perceiving sonic input that resembles our idea of 'a voice' and perceptualizing it into 'a voice.' In such a percept, we sense a moving body, as the vocal tract changes shape to produce resonances mixed with noises, stops, and silences. Through perceptualization, we cognitively represent the body that we hear moving.

Throughout human evolution, this process has proven mostly effective. For example, hearing a cricket on a summer evening reliably indicates the presence of a cricket, making the process of sound source identification unremarkably predictable. On the other hand, the scream of a fox in the darkness of a rural night can be alarming because it resembles a human shriek. Electronically produced sound increases the potential for ambiguity, as the age-old causal logic between the physical source of a sound and our perception of that source is complicated by the possibility that a sound may only be a reproduction or simulation (Fales 2005: 64), emerging from a speaker somewhere outside the field of vision.

The combination of the highly perceptualized nature of formant-based sounds—such as the human voice—and the ability of audio technology to decontextualize sounds from their sources means that twenty-first-century humans are primed to 'hear voices' even when no human body is present. But what factors make a 'human-sounding' voice coming from an electronic device seem unacceptable?

2.4 Audiovisual Uncanny: In a Robot State of Mind

2.4.1 Sound in the Uncanny Valley

In 1970, a short essay by Japanese roboticist Masahiro Mori on the affective aspects of humanoid robots introduced the notion of the uncanny valley—an idea that has not only shaped research in robotics design but also stimulated research in disciplines as far afield as ethics, psychology, neuroscience, and game and animation studies. As designers improved their ability to build human-looking robots (or androids), Mori speculated that, contrary to the assumption that robots would be more appealing to more closely they resembled humans, instead, people's heightened sense of affinity with such machines sharply declined the closer the resemblance, rising again sharply with full human resemblance. Mori dubbed this affective dip the *bukimi no tani*, or uncanny valley [lit. creepy-feeling valley] effect (Mori 2012: 98).

While the figure of a corpse marks the low point of this valley, the effect is intensified when movement taken into account, with the zombie, an animated corpse at the deepest point. Mori's thought experiment included multisensory experience as an experiential, time-based phenomenon, asserting that "because of a variation in movement, something that has come to appear close to human—like a robot, puppet, or prosthetic hand—could easily tumble down into the uncanny valley" (Mori 2012: 100). The effect is like touching a prosthetic hand when expecting a living human one or watching an awkward slowness of an android's smile. Mori proposed that the feeling of sudden unfamiliarity or creepiness can be explained by the uncanny object's closeness to death. We feel uncomfortable as a response to "proximal sources of danger" such as contagion—part of our "instinct for self-preservation" (Mori 2012: 100). Researchers in many fields have studied human reactions to the appearance, movement, and sound of anthropomorphic robots since Mori's initial observations in 1970.

Cognitive scientists MacDorman and Chattopadhyay (2016) propose realism inconsistency rather than category uncertainty as the cause of the sense of uncanniness. Based on an experiment comparing computer-modeled still images of objects and human and animal faces, they posit that the uncanny valley does not originate in psychological discomfort, but from "conflicting—not missing—perceptual cues, which cause prediction error in or between brain areas engaged in automatic, stimulus-driven perceptual processing" (MacDorman and Chattopadhyay 2016: 192). Realism inconsistency theory is compatible with other explanations. What MacDorman and Chattopadhyay describe as "nonhuman features in a humanlike entity" cause the uncanny valley effect by eliciting "large feedback error signals" (MacDorman and Chattopadhyay 2016: 192).

Interestingly, results allow for the possibility that people can become desensitized to the uncanny valley effect.

Perhaps since Mori's initial idea addressed the creepiness of androids' visual appearance exclusively, there is less research examining the uncanny valley effects of robotic and near-human vocalization. Mitchell et al. (2011), a team of scientists studying human-computer interaction (HCI), found that mismatches between appearance and vocal quality elicit the uncanny valley, observing "a robot with a human voice, or a human being with a synthetic voice, will be perceived as eerier than a robot with a synthetic voice or a human being with a human voice" (Mitchell et al. 2011: 11). The team contrasted video loops of a stereotypical robot image (square metal body and mechanical head) and a middle-aged white male human. They recommended that the human realism of a character's visual elements and voice should match (Mitchell et al. 2011: 12) in order to avoid eerie effects in robotics design.

Research in cognitive neuropsychology by Diel and Lewis (2024) points out the lack of conclusive evidence that a synthetic voice without visual stimuli causes the uncanny valley effect. Their paired experiments expand the middle area between synthetic and typically human, including synthesized voices that were "noticeably distorted" and recordings of individual human speakers with "diverse voice pathologies" such as lesions and vocal fold paralysis (Diel and Lewis 2024: 3). Their study results affirm that recordings of human-like voices can stimulate the uncanny valley effect when they sound anomalous, but the researchers also assert that "modern synthetic voices successfully escape a vocal uncanny valley" (Diel and Lewis 2024: 10). Interestingly, Diel and Lewis find that a mismatch of social context and a synthetic voice's expression (i.e., intonation and prosody) can trigger a sense of eeriness (Diel and Lewis 2024: 9). They conclude that uncanniness of voice is best attributed to deviations from listeners' familiar categories rather than to categorical ambiguity—that is, unlike complete unfamiliarity, close resemblance to something known but with a small deviation will trigger the uncanny valley effect (Diel and Lewis 2024: 1).

2.4.2 Talking Movie Monsters

Horror movies exploit the potential of recorded voices to sound creepy. The genre builds on the combination of sound and visuals to create an audiovisual uncanny: exaggerated speech articulation, speech-lip movement asynchrony, and vocalization associated with disturbed emotional states and vicious animals. These categories have been enlisted for their unsettling effects since the advent of sound in film, going so far as to take advantage of weaknesses in the early sound film technology. Spadoni (2007) suggests that the acceptability of recorded dialog depended as much on the "acclimation of individual viewers to sound film as it did on the ongoing improvements in the technology itself" (Spadoni 2007: 14).

The association of monsters with awkward speech delivery goes back to foundational works of sound cinema such as *Dracula* (1931). Tod Browning, the film's director, effectively exploited both the unsettling potential of Bela Lugosi's deep accented voice and the limitations of the recording technology, as actors had to speak clearly and slowly to ensure effective audio recording (Spadoni 2007: 63). Furthermore, Lugosi, the Hungarian stage and silent film actor, was unaccustomed to sound film acting, and delivered his lines with a style that became a hallmark of the classic, creepy 'horror' voice (Spadoni 2007).

On the other end of the spectrum, the eponymous monster in James Whale's 1931 film *Frankenstein* combined a lack of facial expression (resulting from the elaborate makeup necessary for the role) with animalistic vocalizations that emphasize the monster's power and otherness. Just as hearing the sonic similarity of a coyote's howl to a human cry brings us into the uncanny valley, with the sudden realization that there is no clear distinction between humans and other animals.

These early innovations in sound film have become familiar staples in the horror genre, transferring into other audiovisual media. For instance, Tinwell (2015) found that particular vocal qualities influence an audience's empathy with or distance from video game characters: "Speech that was judged to be of the wrong pitch and intonation and monotone speech, without intonation and expressivity … increased the uncanny for a character" (Tinwell 2015: 55).

In addition, sound-image asynchrony—meaning a time lag between what we see and hear in a movie or game—can have an unsettling effect. Human listeners have a high tolerance for slight offset of speech movement and sound, such as is naturally associated with real-life echoey spaces. Tinwell observes: "There is some leverage in our sensitivity to achieve temporal coordination for multisensory signals such as speech and lip movement as a singular event" (Tinwell 2015: 61). However, beyond the "synchrony window" of over 400 milliseconds (Tinwell 2015: 62), people start to consciously notice the lag.

Furthermore, humans are more sensitive to negative asynchrony, meaning that we are more sensitive to a mismatch if an audible voice starts even slightly before we see the associated mouth movements. Average viewers detected a lag in sound at 220 milliseconds with a sound lagging after the image, but only 50 milliseconds when the sound preceded the visual stream (Tinwell 2015). Tinwell hypothesizes that because humans rely on visual as well as aural cues for processing speech, in such cases negative asynchrony means that rather than observing the speaker's lips to help process meaning, we are "distracted by the speech sound and wonder where it is coming from" (Tinwell 2015: 62)—leading to an increased sense of uncanniness. Echoing Mori (2012), she also suggests that speech which is widely asynchronized from lip movement may indicate the utterances of a person who has "lost control of their normal bodily or mental functions" (Tinwell 2015: 64) and may thus be unwell or even dangerous. Conversely, it may indicate that there is something wrong with the listener's perceptual abilities or state of mind.

2.5 Feeling Formants: What Makes a Voice Feel Wrong?

2.5.1 Voices with/out Bodies

Our hearing is extremely attuned to human vocalization—and our sense of what is human depends on what we judge to match a living human's body moving. The sight of android movement may trigger the sense of discomfort known as the uncanny valley effect, depending on how closely it mimics human embodiment. A synthesized or robotic voice is less disturbing than the sound of an organic human voice that is distorted or unfamiliar. When watching and listening to a human vocalizing, slight discrepancies in the sight and sound, irregularities in the physical context that may give warning—the sound of the voice lagging behind the mouth's movement or an utterance that indicates the possibility of illness or violence. While we may adjust our idea of what counts as irregular or dangerous—even learning to love the robotic song of a vocoder—hearing sound nevertheless reflects aspects of material reality, providing information about our surroundings and our own physical forms. Since formants resonate with the internal shape of the vocal mechanism, artificially altering these resonances in ways that defy human possibility will be immediately noticeable.

This effect is most obvious when shifting all harmonics of the voice equally, for example, speeding up (or slowing down) a recording on an analog tape recorder. This alters not only the fundamental F0 frequency of the voice but also its formant frequencies. As the formants shift with the fundamental pitch range, many listeners will perceptualize an impossible distorted human body speaking with a miniscule (if the frequencies are higher) or massive (if they are lower) human-shaped vocal tract. Even when adjusting formants according to accurate mathematical and physiological models, as is possible with Vocaloid, subtle inconsistencies can give listeners clues that the sounds are technological artifacts. Jim Aikin, reviewing the original Miriam vocal library in 2004, critiqued Vocaloid's gender factor parameter, which correctly shifted pitch along with formant peaks to allow users to transform the female voice of the donor into a 'male' voice. For Aikin, the resulting 'male' sound was unconvincing, as if "the vowel formants are being shifted but not the consonants"—leading to a lack of integration between phonetic elements in the overall vocal sound (Aikin 2004).

In short, the social and cultural expectations of listeners, the material contexts of listeners and singers, and physical qualities of the sound all contribute to the uncanny feeling of distorted yet human vocalization.

2.5.2 Paprika *(2006): Susumu Hirasawa's Vocaloid Uncanny*

Two tracks composed by Japanese electropop musician Susumu Hirasawa illustrate how Vocaloid synthesis can sound uncanny by exploiting formant perception. Hirasawa used Yamaha's original Lola and Meiko Vocaloids on his 2006 album *Byakkoya*, with two songs adapted for use in director Satoshi Kon's animated feature, *Paprika* (2006)—one of several collaborations between the two artists (Hirasawa 2008). The plot of the film hinges on the distinction between dreams and reality starting to unravel, and Hirasawa's upbeat, sometimes frenetic tracks underline the comical and grotesque atmosphere of this world (Hirasawa 2007).

Paprika, the protagonist and supernatural alter-ego of female scientist Atsuko Chiba, is linked to one of the film's two main theme songs, "The Girl in Byakkoya" (Hirasawa 2007). Hirasawa's use of the Vocaloid voices reflects Paprika's morphing abilities and the film's overall theme of dreamlike, and sometimes nightmarish, transformations. In the opening scene, the vocals fade in as we see Paprika's name on an illustrated namecard; the music continues throughout the screen's opening titles. From the beginning, this links Paprika to the Vocaloid's repeated lines *"yoiya naze ni mugen to mihai"* [drunken musing on infinity and beauty], repeated in a light-hearted, clearly processed voice. In 2006, this was a unique vocal sound very few people had yet heard. "The Girl"—without Hirasawa's lead vocals—accompanies Paprika on her magical journey through Tokyo as she flies into the air, changes size, and leaps in and out of background animations.

The original "Byakkoya" begins and ends with the same lines sung only in a lower 'male' voice, which begs the question of how Hirasawa (2006) achieved relatively naturalistic vocals with either Lola or Meiko (both voice libraries recorded by female vocalists). This voice's rapidly shifting vowel resonance triggers a visceral sense of the 'singer's' larynx bobbing impossibly up and down as this uncanny singer moves between syllables. In "Byakkoya" as well as in "The Girl," Hirasawa does not attempt to smooth the impossible melodic leaps and flutters in the Vocaloid's repeated melody line. In "The Girl," the widely warbling trill of the high voice is doubled an octave below by the synthesized 'male' vocal of the original song.

During the film's closing credits, we hear a complete reprise of "The Girl" with Hirasawa's own clear tenor singing the verses, both touchstone and foil to the strange backing vocals that continue throughout. The composer's Vocaloid *"baka kōrasu"* [crazy idiot chorus] (Hirasawa 2008) adds a ghostly edge to the otherwise bright tune. The clownish voices contrast with the cleanly plucked synth harpsichord and soaring synth strings. On occasion, the belching Vocaloid chorus blasts a staccato, impossibly precise.

The sense of the vocal body implied by the Vocaloids' repeated verse, shifting in unusual if not impossible ways, reflects exactly the sort of circus-like shape-shifting and nightmarish morphing of Kon's animated narrative. "Parade," the film's second main theme song, which also features the early Vocaloid libraries, accompanies a scene in the film in which the inhabitants of the city go into a carnivalesque frenzy (Hirasawa 2007). Salarymen dive off buildings like synchronized swimmers while household appliances come to life and march down a confetti-filled boulevard (Kon 2006). Humans join the parade only to have their heads morph into dolls, guitars, TVs, or cell phones (Kon 2006). The face of a smiling Japanese doll twists into that of a strangely smiling middle-aged man (Kon 2006).

The bubbly yet disturbing atmosphere of the scene is reflected in the music, including the strange new Vocaloid timbre.

The baritone Vocaloid line with its metallic timbral sheen and awkward vowel shifts comes forth again here, repeating an incomprehensible line (possibly part of a Buddhist sutra) with a pronounced yodeling melody. In "Parade" the crazy chorus again shouts in brief punctuations as a synthesized marching band ramps in on an ascending minor riff. Hirasawa's vivid lyrics deliver an oblique critique of consumer society, which, as "liberty, a parody of utopia," is a "parade of terror" and "madness, coming in your name"[3] (Hirasawa 2007 my translation). Each verse ends with Hirasawa's own voice doubled, the lower octave sung intimately close to the microphone, and the higher melody-line filtered for a whistling lo-fi radio effect. The combination of human and artificial singing on this track creates an uncanny morphing chaos that is in keeping with the dreamlike quality of the film's plot, imagery, and overall theme.

2.5.3 2001: A Space Odyssey *(1968)*: *The Human Voice of Creepy AI*

In contrast to Hirasawa's experimentation with Vocaloid for *Paprika*, the disembodied voice of HAL9000 in Stanley Kubrik's 1968 science fiction classic sounds entirely human. The role is voiced by Canadian stage actor Douglas Rain, with a calm and benign delivery increasingly inappropriate to the dire situations faced by the crew of the Discovery One spacecraft. This uncanny mismatch of vocal emotion and social context is what makes the iconic voice characterization of HAL9000 so effective. HAL's utter calm as he explains with slow, deliberate enunciation the necessity of murder, paired with his panoptic control over the ship, gives him a superhuman quality. This synthetic yet all-too-human intelligence, with failing functionality when faced impossibly contradictory orders, sounds exactly like the psychopath he has become. The studio mixing of the HAL audio track, a very close, dry sound without being incorporated into diegetic locations with reverb or panning further, multiplies his omnipotence. The final, jarring discrepancies between HAL's slow, calm begging for mercy and the gradual slowdown of his final song highlight this film's iconic sound design, showing how an organic human voice can itself symbolize all that we fear about machine intelligence.

---

[3] "*Are ga ribatii, yūtopia no parodii … Kyōfu/kyōki no pareido ga kuru, kimi no na no shita ni*" (Hirasawa 2007).

References

Aikin, Jim. 2004. Zero-G Vocaloid Miriam—Vocal Synthesis Software (PC). *Keyboard*, September 1, 76.

Arai, Takayuki. 2004. History of Chiba and Kajiyama and Their Influence in Modern Speech Science. In *From Sound to Sense: 50+ Years of Discoveries in Speech Communication. Conference Proceedings*. Cambridge, MA: MIT. C115–C120.

Balmont, James. 2023. An Introduction to Ryuichi Sakamoto in Six Albums. *Dazed*, January 19. Accessed 15 December 2023. https://www.dazeddigital.com/music/article/57973/1/a-guide-to-ryuichi-sakamotos-pioneering-sound-in-six-essential-albums

Bell, Sarah. 2024. *Vox Ex Machina*. Cambridge, MA: MIT Press.

Chan, Paul Yaozhu. 2020. *The Psychoacoustics and Synthesis of Singing Harmony*. Doctoral thesis, Nanyang Technological University, Singapore.

Diel, Alexander, and Michael Lewis. 2024. Deviation from Typical Organic Voices Best Explains a Vocal Uncanny Valley. *Computers in Human Behavior Reports* 14:1–15. Accessed 30 June 2024. https://www.sciencedirect.com/science/article/pii/S2451958824000630

Dudley, Homer. 1938. *System for the Artificial Production of Vocal or Other Sounds*. US Patent 2,121,142 filed April 7, 1937, and issued June 21, 1938.

Dudley, Homer. 1939a. *Signal Transmission*. US Patent 2,151,091 filed October 30, 1935, and issued March 21, 1939.

Dudley, Homer. 1939b. Remaking Speech. *The Journal of the Acoustical Society of America* 11 (2): 169–177.

Dudley, Homer. 1940. The Carrier Nature of Speech. *The Bell System Technical Journal* 19 (4): 495–515.

Duinker, Ben. 2025. Auto-Tune as Instrument: Trap Music's Embrace of a Repurposed Technology. *Popular Music*:1–25. https://doi.org/10.1017/S0261143024000369

Fales, Cornelia. 2002. The Paradox of Timbre. *Ethnomusicology* 46 (1): 56–95.

Fales, Cornelia. 2005. Short-circuiting Perceptual Systems: Timbre in Ambient and Techno Music. In *Wired for Sound: Engineering and Technologies in Sonic Cultures*, ed. Paul Greene and Thomas Porcello, 156–180. Middletown CT: Wesleyan University Press.

Fant, Gunnar. 1960. *Acoustic Theory of Speech Production: With Calculations Based on X-Ray Studies of Russian Articulations*. The Hague, Netherlands: DeGruyter.

Fant, Gunnar. 2001. T Chiba and M Kajiyama: Pioneers in Speech Acoustics. *Speech, Music and Hearing: Quarterly Progress Report* 42 (1): 59–60.

Fant, Gunnar. 2004. Phonetics and Phonology in the Last 50 Years: Speech Research in a Historical Perspective. In *From Sound to Sense: 50+ Years of Discoveries in Speech Communication. Conference Proceedings*. Cambridge, MA: MIT. B20–B41.

Fujii, Takeshi. 2019. *YMO no Ongaku* [The Music of YMO]. Tokyo: Artes Publishing.
Hirasawa, Susumu. 2006. *Byakkoya* [White Tiger Field]. CD. Tokyo: Chaos Union, CHTE-0034.
Hirasawa, Susumu. 2007. *Paprika (Music from the Motion Picture)*. CD. Los Angeles: Milan Records, M2-36284.
Hirasawa, Susumu. 2008. Bācharuna 'Josei' e no Yokubō to ha Nanika. [What is This Desire for a Virtual 'Woman'?] Interview by Tomita Akihiro. *Eureka: Shi to Sōtokushū: Hatsune Miku Netto ni Maifurita Tenshi* 40 (15): 95–105.
Holmes, Thom. 2020. *Electronic and Experimental Music: Technology, Music, and Culture*. 6th ed. New York: Routledge.
Jude, Gretchen. 2018. Vocal Performance Through Electrical Flows: Making Current Kin. *Performance Philosophy* 4 (2): 393–409.
Kon, Satoshi. 2006. *Paprika*. Motion Picture. Screenplay by Seishi Minakami and Satoshi Kon. Sony Pictures Entertainment Japan.
Kubrik, Stanley. 1968. *2001: A Space Odyssey*. Motion Picture. Screenplay by Stanley Kubrick and Arthur C. Clarke. Warner Bros. Pictures.
Kubrik, Stanley. 1971. *A Clockwork Orange*. Motion Picture. Screenplay by Stanley Kubrick. Warner Bros. Pictures.
MacDorman, Karl, and Dabaleena Chattopadhyay. 2016. Reducing Consistency in Human Realism Increases the Uncanny Valley Effect; Increasing Category Uncertainty Does Not. *i-Cognition* 146:190–205.
Manning, Peter. 2013. *Electronic and Computer Music*. 4th ed. Oxford, UK: Oxford University Press.
Mills, Mara. 2012. Media and Prosthesis: The Vocoder, the Artificial Larynx, and the History of Signal Processing. *Qui Parle: Critical Humanities and Social Sciences* 21 (1): 107–149.
Mitchell, Wade, Kevin Szerszen, Lu Amy Shiron, Paul Schermerhorn, Matthias Scheutz, and Karl MacDorman. 2011. A Mismatch in the Human Realism of Face and Voice Produces an Uncanny Valley. *i-Perception* 2 (1): 10–12. Accessed 2 January 2017. https://journals.sagepub.com/doi/10.1068/i0415.
Mori, Masahiro. 2012. The Uncanny Valley. Transl. Karl F. MacDorman and Norri Kageki. *IEEE Robotics & Automation Magazine*: June edition.
Pickett, J. M. 1999. *The Acoustics of Speech Communication: Fundamentals, Speech Perception Theory, and Technology*. Needham Heights, MA: Allyn & Bacon.
Pisanski, Katarzyna, and Gregory Bryant. 2019. The Evolution of Voice Perception. In *The Oxford Handbook of Voice Studies*, eds. Nina Sun Eidsheim and Katherine Meizel, 269–300. Oxford: Oxford University Press. https://doi.org/10.1093/oxfordhb/9780199982295.013.36
Rachel, Elkind-Tourre. 2000. *Wendy Carlos*. Website. Accessed 15 December 2024. https://www.wendycarlos.com/rachel.html

Smith, Julius. 2010. *Physical Audio Signal Processing for Virtual Musical Instruments and Digital Audio Effects.* Stanford: W3K Publishing.
Spadoni, Robert. 2007. *Uncanny Voices in Early Cinema: The Coming of Sound Film and the Origins of the Horror Genre.* Berkeley, CA: University of California Press.
Stewart, John W. 1972. Obituaries: John Q. Stewart. *Physics Today* 25 (6): 75.
Story, Brad. 2019. History of Speech Synthesis. In *Routledge Handbook of Phonetics*, ed. William Katz and Peter Assmann, 9–33. London: Routledge.
Sundberg, Johan. 1978. Synthesis of Singing. *Swedish Journal of Music Research* 60 (1): 107–112.
Sundberg, Johan. 2007. Synthesising Singing. In *Proceedings, 4th Sound and Music Computing Conference, Lefkada, Greece.*
Tinwell, Angela. 2015. *The Uncanny Valley in Games and Cinema.* Boca Raton, FL: CRC Press.
Yellow Magic Orchestra. 1979. *Solid State Survivor.* CD. Tokyo: Alfa Records: ALR 6022.
Yellow Magic Orchestra. 2000. *YMO 1979 Transatlantic Tour.* DVD. Tokyo: Toshiba EMI: TOBF-5024.

CHAPTER 3

From Daisy to Miku: Digital Voices in the Information Age

Abstract This chapter gives an account of how Arthur C. Clarke found inspiration for the character of HAL9000, the infamous computer intelligence, in the world's first digitally synthesized singing, which he encountered at Bell Labs in the early 1960s. The chapter then gives a brief overview of two key mathematical concepts, the Nyquist limit and the Fourier series, which both facilitated the development of digital audio and advanced voice synthesis methods. Several notable singing voice synthesis systems from the 1980s through the early 2000s are introduced leading to a detailed focus on the development of Vocaloid. The Vocaloid synthesis engine up to Vocaloid 6 utilized concatenative synthesis, with voicebanks (also known as voice libraries, databases, and vocal fonts) provided by several companies. The chapter distinguishes between audio sampling and signal sampling in order to clarify how concatenative synthesis, although relying on large databases of recordings, is different from audio sampling. A case study of the first song released using Vocaloid singing synthesis is examined as a case study to highlight early limitations of the product's sound. The chapter compares Version 1 and Version 2 voicebanks, designed and marketed by two difference companies. It concludes with an examination of design aspects of the Vocaloid's first character voice, Hatsune Miku, emphasizing the importance of the product's nonmusical elements.

Keywords Inspiration for HAL9000 • *Illiac Suite for String Quartet* (1957) • "Bicycle Built for Two" (1962) • IBM 7094 • Max Mathews' MUSIC N • Digital singing synthesis (1980–2000) • Hideki Matsutake's Vocaloid song • Zero-G Vocaloid products • Crypton Future Media • Hatsune Miku voice donor

3.1 How the First Singing Computer Made Cinema History: Bell Labs, 1961

When Arthur C. Clarke, the mathematician and author of *2001: A Space Odyssey*, reflected upon the inspiration for the character of HAL9000, he inadvertently misremembered details of computer music history (Clarke xiv, 1998). Clarke famously chose "Daisy Bell (Bicycle Built for Two)," a popular song from the late nineteenth century (Dacre 1892), as the tune sung by the malfunctioning sentient artificial intelligence HAL as it nears deactivation. But Clarke wrote this scene after a visit to Bell Telephone Laboratories in the early 1960s, where he heard a computer rendition of the tune—a feat he recalls as "a recording of an Illiac computer singing" (Clarke xiv, 1998). The confusion is understandable, given that Clarke's former Cambridge classmate taught at the University of Illinois at Urbana-Champagne from the early 1950s to the early 1970s, the same time period and place where the ILLIAC (Illinois Automatic Computer) series was developed. One of the most powerful computers of its time, ILLIAC I, was used by composer Lejaren Hiller (with mathematician Leonard Isaacson) to generate the music score for *Illiac Suite for String Quartet* in the mid-1950s (Hiller and Isaacson 1959). It is important to note that ILLIAC I did not synthesize audio output for this piece; rather, the computer generated a score for human players to perform. Nevertheless, the computer's groundbreaking accomplishments impressed Clarke enough that he later made Urbana, Illinois, the "birthplace" of the artificial intelligence he christened Heuristically Programmed Algorithmic Computer—better known as HAL. HAL9000's 1968 rendition of "Daisy Bell" became a touchstone in cultural memory through Clarke's novel and Stanley Kubrik's classic sci-fi film, both results of their collaboration.

The inspiration for HAL's iconic swansong was released as "Bicycle Built for Two" in 1962, with M.V. Mathews credited for arrangement and the IBM 7094 credited for audio output of both synthesized voice and synthesized piano (Music from Mathematics 1962). The project was initiated at Bell Labs in 1961, using Mathews' groundbreaking MUSIC "computer music rendering" language (Puckette 2020: 63–64). Influential music software developer Miller Puckette later extended the credit for this groundbreaking work—the first singing generated by a computer—to acknowledge both Max V. Mathews and Joan Miller[1] (Puckette 2020). Bell Labs' digital-to-analog sound transducer, a 12-bit vacuum tube converter that generated an audio wave from a stream of numbers recorded on magnetic tape, was the first of its kind (Roads 1980). This audio converter, along with physical modeling software, is the innovation that first made a computer sing, and MUSIC III voiced the song that Clarke heard—with the software running on IBM's 704 and 7094 mainframes that were used to develop the MUSIC I-V series between the mid-1950s and the late 1960s (Roads 1980). The software that enabled the computation of the 'voice' sound, created at Bell Labs by John L. Kelly and Carol Lochbaum in 1961, was a digitized vocal tract model that incorporated data from Gunnar Fant's book on vowels—what Smith calls "most likely the first digital physical-modeling synthesis example by any method" (Smith 2010: 453).

3.2 Between Time and Frequency: The Significance of Mathematics in Digital Audio

3.2.1 *Speed and Sound: The Nyquist Limit*

The mechanical designs of early modern inventors such as Kempelen could not replicate the subtle complexity of the function of the human vocal mechanism, although intensive scientific study of human vocalization led to many breakthroughs. By the early twentieth century, audio technology had provided the means to record and play back increasingly real-to-life reproductions of voice recordings. Innovations in electrical transmission and audio circuitry enabled rudimentary voice synthesis, with Homer Dudley's voder allowing a keyboard operator to manually create intelligible speech, circumventing vocal input completely; musicians' creative uses of Dudley's vocoder acclimatized listeners' ears to more unusual voice-like

---

[1] Joan Miller was Mathews' close associate at Bell Labs, a statistician and coder to whom Mathews attributes some of the most complicated code in the Music V program. According to Mathews, Miller focused on the textual aspects of the synthesis, making a smaller contribution to the musical aspects (Park 2009).

sounds. By the early 1960s, digital voice synthesis was becoming a reality. However, high-quality digital audio recording and playback did not become available to consumers until the early 1980s (Immink 1998).

One of the fundamental requirements for digital generation of sound is how fast the system can operate. As Max Mathews observes, "Any sound the human can hear, you can make with the right number, accuracy, and combination of samples, so the computer is a universal instrument" (Park 2009: 11). To digitally reproduce or synthesize a soundwave, the sampling rate (the number of times per second that a continuous analog signal is measured and converted from discrete digital data) must be sufficiently high.

The Nyquist-Shannon Theorem was first proposed in the late 1920s by Harry Nyquist for improving telegraph transmissions and elaborated by Claude Shannon for application to digital systems. It defines the minimum sampling limit required to obtain accurate reconstruction of a signal. The theorem states that a system must sample (measure) at a rate of at least twice the highest frequency in the signal to ensure that it can be reconstituted without aliasing distortion. For example, since the typical human can hear frequencies of up to 20,000 Hz, signal sampling must occur at least 40,000 times per second to accurately reproduce all frequencies up to 20 kHz. As a result, in preparation for mass-production of digital recordings, Sony and Philips, the two companies collaborating on the technology, set the standard for CD quality audio at 44.1 kHz in 1980 (Immink 1998). If the sample rate is lower, then high-frequency information risks being misrepresented as lower frequencies, resulting in aliasing—distortion that introduces unwanted sounds not present in the original signal (Smith 2007).

3.2.2 *Fourier Transforms in the Digital Era*

Jean-Baptiste Joseph Fourier (1768–1830) was best known in his time for his research into heat transfer. His mathematical innovations, particularly his development of the Fourier series, have also been foundational in fields such as data processing and digital music (Fourier 2008; Fourier's Transformational 2018). Fourier's work was crucial in understanding that any complex vibrational waveform could be broken down into a sum of sine waves[2]—an idea applied by Helmholtz to the study of acoustics and aural perception. The Fourier series led to the development of Fourier analysis, which has been widely applied in signal processing, including the manipulation of audio signals for tasks such as analog filtering and spectral analysis. Applications of his ideas were limited until digital computers boosted calculation speed and complexity, but Fourier analysis played a key role in the development of amplitude modulation (AM) and frequency modulation (FM) in analog technologies like radio transmission.

With the advent of computers, Fourier analysis can be used to break down and resynthesize, or transform, any signal. This has facilitated processing the massive amounts of data that are increasingly central to every realm of science, from astronomy to crystallography—including audio (Fourier's Transformational ... 2018). Fourier transforms,[3] such as those used in digital audio, take samples of sound over time and mathematically convert them into a representation of frequency and amplitude at each sample point. Science educator Kalid Azad describes the capability of a Fourier transform as "given a smoothie, it finds the recipe" (Azad 2017). This allows for resynthesis of the original signal as well as manipulation of its spectral content. Once a soundwave has been converted into a stream of numerical data, it can be mathematically processed to produce a wide range of effects, such as distortion, pitch and formant shifting, reverb, and echo modeling, audible when transduced back into the acoustic world. With such a wide range of potential manipulations, how is a digital 'voice' synthesized to be coherently perceptible as human vocal sound?

3.3 OTHER DIGITAL SINGERS: BEFORE VOCALOID

The shifting technological capabilities and sociocultural contexts of the 1980s stimulated new developments in vocal synthesis tools, laying the groundwork for the later successes of Vocaloid. The desire to build upon previous successes and refine existing synthesis capabilities led to research combining previous models (physical and spectral) and vocal modalities (speech and singing). Some research projects were housed and funded by

---

[2] Smith (2011) credits Swiss mathematicians Daniel Bernoulli for the idea and Leonard Euler for notating it in a mathematical formula (Smith 2011).
[3] For example, discrete time Fourier transform (DTFT), fast Fourier transform (FFT), discrete Fourier transform (DFT), short-time Fourier transform (STFT); see Smith (2011) for detailed explanations of these equations applied specifically to audio processing.

prestigious academic institutions such as IRCAM (Paris) and CCRMA (Stanford University in California), but as personal computers and home recording studios became affordable in the late 1990s, the profitability of this specialized technology attracted the investment of corporations such as Texas Instruments.

3.3.1 CHANT

In the late 1970s, just as digital audio tools were poised to advance with more powerful computer technology, researchers at IRCAM (Institute for Research and Coordination in Acoustics/Music) in Paris were developing CHANT, a formant-based, synthesis-by-rule program, initially created to produce sung vowels (Rodet et al. 1984; Bennett and Rodet 1989; Rodet 2002). CHANT automated vowel synthesis, allowing greater focus on musical and expressive parameters; the synthesis of consonants, being more complex and less predictable, required more attention (Bennett and Rodet 1989). Designed for use as an interactive instrument, even the most basic version of CHANT allowed control of over one hundred parameters, including vibrato, random variations of the F0, hoarseness, and intensity of the sound (Bennett and Rodet 1989). As Bennett and Rodet point out, how loudly a singer sings and in what part of their range greatly affect the vocal timbre: "When a vocalist sings loudly, the signal emitted from the vocal cords is completely different from that produced when the vocalist sings softly. It happens that this loud signal is much richer in high frequencies" (27). This product seems to have been aimed at synthesizing European classical vocals, as Xavier Rodet's vowel-only demo of Mozart's "Queen of the Night" aria illustrates (Singing Synthesis 2012).

3.3.2 SPASM

In the 1990s, as personal computers and graphical user interfaces became widely available, singing synthesis research also progressed. The Singing Physical Articulatory Synthesis Model, or SPASM, first introduced by Perry Cook working at Stanford's CCRMA (Center for Computer Research in Music and Acoustics) in 1993, was based on a physical model of the vocal tract—what Cook called "a direct descendent of the Kelly and Lochbaum model, but with many enhancements, such as a nasal tract, modelling of radiation through the throat wall … and real-time control" (Cook 1996: 41). SPASM was based on vocal production mechanisms rather than perception of vocal output as the basis for modeling, as did the formant-based MUSSE and CHANT systems (Cook 1996). For Cook, physical models had more intuitive appeal for users than did spectral models: "Since descriptions of unnatural-sounding synthesized sounds often rely on physical references ('She sounds like her jaw is open too far,' or 'His tongue sounds fat'), the physical parameters indicate what to do to the model controls if the synthesis does not sound correct" (1993: 43).

3.3.3 Lyricos

By 1997, a group of academic and corporate researchers developed a singing synthesis system, Lyricos, based on a method called concatenative, or unit selection, synthesis. This method of digital synthesis relies on rapid selection and processing of short, recorded audio segments from large databases, which are then linked to form longer, more complex streams of sound. This approach is data-driven not rule-based, as the sound is "induced from the data itself" (Schwarz 2006: 4) rather than being created based on pre-determined rules. Concatenative synthesis is "thus a way to replace a large and complicated set of rules by implicit rules from the best performers" (Rodet qtd. in Schwarz 2006: 8).

The Lyricos system applied text-to-speech synthesis to create singing controlled by MIDI-based composition software (Macon et al. 1997: 3). The voice data collection consisted of recordings made for the project by a male classical singer, singing at high and low pitches of 500 nonsense "words" designed to provide a range of "coarticulation effects," meaning the sounds of consonants that can bleed into the sound of a vowel. One example of a coarticulation effect would be the difference in the 'r' sounds of the phrase "are you really?": slowly say the 'ah-r' and 'ree' in sequence and you can hear the effect of the preceding and following vowels on the 'r' sounds.

The 'words' were analyzed, tagged, and divided into 'units' according to phoneme and context for the most natural sound for the sequence of units to be selected, reordered, and smoothed for any differences between the sounds of units at the segment boundaries. The system's computations were based on a sinusoidal model[4] relying on the inverse fast Fourier

---

[4] Specifically, the ABSOLA, or Analysis by Synthesis Overlap and Add sinusoidal model, an early variant of the still-common PSOLA or Pitch Synchronous Overall and Add technique (Macon et al. 1997).

transform to maintain formant structure and enhance overall 'naturalness' of the resulting synthesized voice output. Various parameters in singing quality such as vibrato, pitch, syllabic rhythm, and "vocal effort dynamics" (similar to CHANT's vocal intensity control) were controllable by a "graphical input device" (Macon et al. 1997: 7), although despite the joint development including Texas Instruments and the "industry standard" MIDI control language, Lyricos, one of the earliest musical uses of concatenative synthesis (Schwarz 2006), did not make it to commercial markets.

3.3.4 CataRT

IRCAM researcher Diemo Schwarz proposed a concatenative music synthesis program called Caterpillar in 2000, adding "artistic text-to-speech" synthesis in Talkapillar by 2004 (Beller et al. 2005; Schwarz 2005). IRCAM's CataRT project enriched the real-time synthesis capabilities of previous iterations of this program with granular synthesis, a technique which creates 'clouds' of sound by playing back layers of very short samples ('grains') of a sound file with various adjustments (i.e., changed pitch, volume, or playback direction) (Schwarz 2006). Schwarz's team found the interactive potential of granular synthesis to be an "inspiration" for CataRT (Schwarz et al. 2006: DAFX2). Their interest in interactivity and more intuitive forms of user control of this program is evident in the aim to allow gestural control of the sound via a graphics tablet—an uncommon device at the time (Schwarz et al. 2006: DAFX5). While the system was not aimed primarily at voice synthesis, work at IRCAM in the early and mid-2000s reflected the approach of the Yamaha collaboration. Schwarz also forecasted the limits of data-driven concatenative synthesis as being not a lack of digital content to choose from but difficulty managing such large amounts of data (Schwarz 2007: 104)—a challenge made obsolete by advances in artificial intelligence systems a decade later.

3.3.5 CANTOR

In 2004, VirSyn, a German digital music effects and apps developer, released CANTOR, their formant-based singing synthesis product. The company's "virtual instrument" replaced the filters of MUSSE with sinusoids that replicated formants; vowel templates could be stored so that the user could "specify how to morph between them" (Chan 2020: 65). As

Conner (2013) points out, "[T]hough it offered musical voice synthesis comparable to the Yamaha software it was more expensive and required more difficult commercial licensing than Vocaloid. A final version of CANTOR was released in 2007, and it has not since been updated" (Conner 60fn).[5] CANTOR focused on European classical singing timbre, which may have limited the scope of potential audiences and users.

3.4 From Concatenation to the Miku Phenomenon: What's in a Database?

3.4.1 A Brief History of Vocaloid

In March 2000, researchers from Yamaha, one of the world's largest musical instrument and audio equipment companies, joined computer scientists at the Music Technology Group (MTG) at Spain's prestigious Pompeu Fabra University to inaugurate the Daisy Project—later known as Vocaloid (Kenmochi and Fujimoto 2014). According to computer scientist Àlex Loscos, the project had its origins in Yamaha's Elvis Project, which between 1997 and 2000 prototyped a product that could transform a karaoke singer's voice in real time, replacing its timbre with a celebrity singer's vocals (Loscos 2019). Although the Elvis product never went on the market, the connection between MTG scientists and Yamaha remained strong.

The Daisy Project aimed to bring to the audio market what Hideki Kenmochi, developer and "father of Vocaloid," initially approached as "a very specialised music production tool"—a product designed for digital musicians who wanted to create songs but lacked a singer (Hernández 2020: 20). The team's initial approach combined the strengths of spectral and physical modeling into a "pseudophysical model" (Bonada et al. 2001) that was based on concatenative synthesis (Bonada and Loscos 2003).

This singing synthesis model was influenced by previous computer music research, such as spectral modeling synthesis (SMS) developed at Stanford's CCRMA, where Xavier Serra, the founder of the Music Technology Group, had earned his doctorate (Serra and Smith 1990; Loscos 2019). It was also rooted in systems that, since the early 1970s, had applied multiple Fourier transforms to musical synthesis (Serra and Smith 1990). In 2001, the team presented their elaborated source-filter

---

[5] As of February 2, 2025, Virsyn's CANTOR website certificate was expired.

model, in which "model parameters are extracted from real voice sounds that have been analyzed with SMS" then processed through their EpR (excitement plus resonance) filter sequence, with the first filter modeling a glottal pulse and the second modeling vocal tract resonance (Bonada et al. 2001). The computationally intensive processes of the synthesis module relied on two databases, one storing timbre (samples of voiced phonemes at different pitches and dynamics) and another holding voice information (including templates of vocal characteristics, such as vibrato, based on sample analysis data). Both databases required hours of high-quality audio data recorded by a skilled singer. The spectral modeling synthesis system was controlled using a rule-based "expressiveness module" that included both musical parameters (i.e., pitch) and vocal characteristics (i.e., note release).

By early 2003, the digital singing software was ready for public promotion (Takahashi 2011). Before the team could submit a press release to the (now-defunct) Musikmesse music industry trade fair in Frankfurt, Germany, Daisy Project's product needed a new name. There was some excitement about the possibility of "Ebeamo," after a regionally famous vegetable dish popular near Yamaha's Toyooka site in Shizuoka, Japan (Kenmochi and Fujimoto 2014: 55). However, team leader at Yamaha Hideki Fujii, reflecting on how close they were to the dream of approaching a human voice, captured the feeling of "something vocal-like" but with a robotic nuance with an internationally accessible name: VOCALOID (Kenmochi and Fujimoto 2014: 54, my translation). Following praise of UK company Zero-G's releases of English-language Vocaloid products Lola and Leon[6] in early 2004 (with Miriam released a few months later), Japan's Crypton Future Media brought out two Japanese voice libraries, Meiko and Kaito. The software received positive reviews in Western trade press, winning Electronic Musician magazine's Editor's Choice Award for Most Innovative Product (Takahashi 224). However, unsurprisingly it was in Japan that Vocaloid initially made the most impact. Electronic musicians Hideki Matsutake, well-known for his work with YMO and Isao Tomita, and Susumu Hirasawa were both excited by the possibilities of singing synthesis software, both composing songs using the original Vocaloid engine in the mid-2000s. In 2006, Russian producer Alexei Ustinov's experiments with the Leon vocal font resulted in an album

[6] Musicologist Nina Eidsheim (2018) analyzes the marketing and racialized timbre of these "virtual soul singers" in *The Race of Sound*.

release: *Mesto Pod Solncem* [A Place in the Sun], although it remains out of print as of early 2025.

The rise of Internet sharing platforms and the development of the Character Vocal Series marketed by Hokkaido-based Crypton Future Media made Vocaloid 2 (V2) an exponentially bigger success than its predecessor. In late August 2007, the Hatsune Miku voice library was released, accompanied by a striking image of the digital singer herself, drawn by illustrator KEI to evoke a sense of cuteness and innocence (Hernández 2020: 41–42). The Japanese kanji characters chosen to write "*hatsune*" (lit. first sound). Her name is famously translated as "first sound of the future," although "*miku*" (which, in Japanese naming convention, would be her given name) is written using the katakana phonetic script, which leaves the name open to multiple interpretations and word play. One example is the Project DIVA 39's Giving Day solo concert at Zepp Tokyo on March 9, 2010. The 3 and 9 can be pronounced both as "*mi-ku*" (for Miku) and as "*san-ku*" (which, followed by '*s*,' sounds equivalent, to Japanese ears, to the English word 'thanks'). The set list for the show comprised exactly 39 songs (Takahashi 2011: 7).

Within three months, the Character Vocal Series was being described as a "revolution" in Japan's DIY DeskTop Music (DTM) world (Hernández 2020: 41). Before the release of the V2 Hatsune Miku software, the Vocaloid development team considered scrapping the project due to lukewarm sales; within a year, the product had sold 40,000 copies—over ten times the successful sales record of Vocaloid in 2004 (Hernández 2020: 41). An entire community of independent content producers (often remaining anonymous or pseudonymous) shared songs on NicoNico Douga[7] (an online media-sharing platform similar to YouTube)—an emergent cultural shift that researchers from Japan's National Institute of Advanced Industrial Science and Technology dubbed a "massively collaborative creation community via the Web" (Hamasaki et al. 2009: 222). The appeal of the software moved beyond the popular and DIY music with Steve Hui's digital opera, *The Memory Palace of Matteo Ricci*, commissioned by the 2010 New Vision Arts Festival in Hong Kong (Young 2013).

The year 2011 saw the release of Vocaloid 3, with a newly recorded English-language voicebank for Hatsune Miku, as international interest in the phenomenon grew, first making waves outside the world of Japanese

---

[7] Rebranded as Niconico Inc. in 2012.

pop culture fans. Character Vocals became available not only in English and Japanese but also in Korean, Spanish, and Chinese. In November 2012, Grammy-nominated composer and electronic music pioneer Isao Tomita premiered his *Symphony Ihatov* at Tokyo Opera City Concert Hall (Shiba 2014); the work featured the Japan Philharmonic along with adult and children's choruses (of over 300 human performers), accompanying real-time Hatsune Miku computer graphics and Vocaloid commands synchronized by a human computer musician following the human conductor (Kurita 2014). Composer Keiichiro Shibuya—following the success of his Vocaloid opera, *THE END*, in Japan in late 2012 and 2013—staged *THE END* in November 2013 at Paris's Théâtre du Châtelet, the first of multiple performances across Europe (Shiba 2014).

Yamaha released Vocaloid 4 in 2014, with new voicebanks for more variety and multimedia features facilitating Miku's (and other Character Vocals') global popularity (Shiba 2014). Mobile apps and gaming features of Vocaloid 5, released in 2018, improved the user interface and came bundled with four voicebanks (with four more added with Premium version), rather than requiring separate purchase of vocal libraries. Vocaloid's 2022 release of Vocaloid:AI added capability for the user to create original libraries based on their own voice input as well as multiple new voicebanks, using AI (New Developed AI 2022). As of 2025, there were over one hundred official voice libraries available in five languages (Japanese, English, Mandarin, Korean, and Spanish). Vocaloid's capability to synthesize human-like singing, along with its ease of use and reasonable cost, has made Yamaha's singing voice synthesis software remain an unparalleled success with lasting, widespread cultural impact.

3.4.2 *Yamaha's Vocaloid Engine: Sampling Versus Synthesis*

Concatenative synthesis challenges the traditional distinction between synthesized sound—created by algorithmic models—and sampled sound, which involves playing back (and sometime manipulating) short snippets of existing recorded music. The distinction between synthesis and sampling is increasingly blurred due to the nature of digital audio technology, and the use of the same term, 'sampling,' to describe two different processes. In reality, all digital sound is constructed through the same fundamental process: signal sampling. Digital signal sampling entails capturing measurements of a waveform at regular intervals (standardized at a sample rate of least 44.1 Hz) for storage and playback.

Concatenative synthesis complicates this distinction because, since the approach relies on an extensive database of recorded voice samples, it could be seen as simply playing back a person's voice chopped up and remixed—a more complex version of music sampling, which is ubiquitous in popular genres such as hip-hop. This confusion arises in descriptions of Vocaloid software, with claims that the first version of Vocaloid's synthesis engine was "based off analytics of the human voice," whereas Vocaloid 2 "sample[d] actual human voices" (Suzuki qtd. in St. Michel 2014). Yet the scientists who developed concatenation do not describe it this way. Concatenative synthesis is far more computationally complex than digital audio sampling because it involves analyzing the recordings provided by a singer in multiple ways, then resynthesizing various parameters of that data through algorithmic processing and user input.

While each new version of Vocaloid has improved both synthesis engine and user control, a high-quality recorded database of a skilled singer, "created from dry and noiseless recordings" to provide "both phonetic and expression information" (Bonada and Loscos 2003: 2), has been a fundamental part of Vocaloid from its inception. Those voice sounds provide raw data to create model parameters through extraction and analysis (Bonada et al. 2001). Additionally, the vocal data requires extensive marking and organization prior to inclusion in a singer library.

The V2 synthesis engine, for example, controlled via piano-roll style score editor, converted user-input lyrics into phonetic symbols. From this input, the synthesis engine would select sample units from the singer library for concatenation (Kenmochi 2010). The singer database contained recordings of a special script sung at various pitches, covering all necessary consonant-vowel combinations (called diphones). For Japanese singing synthesis, 500 diphones were necessary, whereas for English the number required was 2500 (Kenmochi 2010).

Extracting diphones rather than isolated phonemes for a voice database yields better synthesis results due to a phenomenon called coarticulation. Coarticulation refers to the slight variations in a phoneme that occur as articulators, such as lips or tongue move to anticipate the next sound or shift from the previous sound (Pickett 1999). Speech synthesis research has found that the middle of a phoneme is "its acoustically most stable region" so using diphones as facilitates smoothing the combination of recorded segments into longer utterance (Pickett 1999: 331). The Vocaloid Version 3 synthesis engine improved voice realism by also incorporating triphones, so that, for instance, an h sound, typically an unvoiced consonant, becomes voiced when surrounded by vowels (Kenmochi 2012).

Once unit samples are selected, the concatenation engine adjusts the pitch of selected diphones, then smooths any differences in timbre between diphones and (by V3) triphones (Kenmochi 2012). In this way, "the original timbre of a sustained vowel is not used but generated by interpolation of the surrounding samples' timbres" (Kenmochi 2012: 5387). This process shows that explanations of Vocaloid that distinguish between "analytics" of a voice and the "actual" human voice samples are insufficient for understanding the function of any version of Vocaloid's concatenative singing synthesis engine. While the user features such as interface and expressive control have been improved and expanded in later versions, concatenation was the basis of the Vocaloid synthesis engine until the release of its AI product in 2022. The special sound of singing voice synthesis by unit concatenation—as distinct from a recorded human voice—was obvious from the start.

3.4.3 From "Daisy" to "That Wonderful Love, Once More": Vocaloid's Real First Sound

In 2003, a year prior to the software's official release, electronic musician, programmer, and composer Hideki Matsutake, widely known as the unofficial fourth member of YMO and apprentice of electronic music composer Isao Tomita, used a prerelease version of Vocaloid software to compose an entirely synthesized cover of songwriter Kazuhiko Katō and Osamu Kitayama's 1971 folk-rock hit "Ano Subarashii Ai Wo Mō Ichidō" [That Wonderful Love, Once More] (Logic System 2003). Judging by the sound, Matsutake appears to have had access to prototypes of the Meiko and Kaito databases, although in the CD liner notes, Matsutake credits the "main vocalist" as "Yamaha's 'Vocaloid'" (Logic System 2003).

In "Ano Subarashii," the software voice sings a straightforward rendition of a heartfelt love song. The synthesized vocals are embedded in layers of instrumental synths and soft, rhythmic noise bursts, with a mellow backbeat that provides a forgiving sonic bed that softens the robotic awkwardness and timbral glitchiness of the prototype software. The first verse is sung solo by a lower 'male' voice—likely the voicebank (provided by Fūga Naoto) that would be commercially released over two years later as the Kaito library; the higher voice is modeled on the prototype Meiko voicebank (provided by Haigo Meiko), one of Crypton Future Media's original Vocaloid Version 1 releases (Takahashi 2011).

The main vocal, floating above a bed of layered synths, sounds smoothly humanoid. But about two minutes into the four-and-a-half-minute song, with the higher voice joining in, an unsettling moment occurs. At 1:44, all the instrumentals drop out (aside from a staticky white-noise pulse keeping the beat), leaving the two synthesized voices duet a cappella for half a verse. In just five seconds, the differences between these singers and human voices become obvious, audible through several elements: the distinctly metallic quality in the higher Vocaloid, the lack of organic smoothness in the pitch glides of the melody line, and the slight lisp of the lower Vocaloid on the final 'sh' sound of the important word *subarashii* [wonderful]—with too little high frequency content in the white noise of last sibilant compared to the 'su' phoneme at the beginning of the word. Once the sustaining synthesizers return and the song regains its relative calm, with the final verse and chorus returning to a relatively pleasant rendition of the song that includes a predictable key modulation and multiple voices harmonizing in the song's final minutes. From a 1961 computer's cover of an 1892 song, Daisy's sound at last came to full fruition in 2003.

3.5   Vocaloid 2: Donor and Design

3.5.1   *Vocaloid 2: The DIY History Behind Miku's Appearance*

The initial reviews of Vocaloid 1, with Yamaha's Vocaloid engine packaged with Zero-G's Vocaloid products (Lola, Leon and, later, Miriam), were positive. A *Sound on Sound* review describing its capabilities as both "impressive" and "remarkable" with the obvious use of the software being for backing vocals (Walden 2004). A review in *Popular Science* positively distinguished Vocaloid from vocoder sound, gushing that the software "does an uncanny job of mimicking the human voice" (Yamaha Vocaloid 2003). Jim Aitken of *Keyboard* was less enthusiastic, pointing out limitations in both ease of use and quality of sound, but encouraging about the overall potential of the product, writing: "The software is difficult to use, but the program is capable of some very interesting things that have been unavailable up until now, certainly at these prices" (Aitken 2004).

Yet for all that Vocaloid 1 succeeded in providing access to singing synthesis capabilities for amateur and professional musicians alike, the technology didn't take off until Version 2—along with the release of the new

Hatsune Miku product by Sapporo-based Crypton Future Media. The design and marketing of Vocaloid 2 with Miku not only allowed users to compose songs with the software but also gave them permission to create and freely share original images of the virtual singer. The combination of this new audiovisual creative tool and burgeoning online video sharing platforms, primarily Japan's NicoNico Douga, fueled a nationwide phenomenon that went global.

Of the two original V1 Japanese voicebanks, Meiko had been far more successful, at least partly attributed to the manga-style avatar on the packaging, which Kaito did not have (Shiba 2014). Crypton's concept for the Character Vocal Series, complete with specific visual and character design choices, ensured that the Miku product would be appealing beyond the product's sound. Not only was the Miku illustration cute without being overtly sexy (Hernández 2020), everything from her hair color to her clothing paid homage to previous electropop and home studio musician—appealing to the so-called DTM (desktop computer music) and DIY culture makers of the 1980s and 1990s, a generation of which Crypton President Hiroyuki Ito was a part. Miku's short skirt is adorned with the small but distinctive pattern of the DIN-5 socket most famously used on early MIDI in-out cables. The black armband on her left arm shows the control panel for Yamaha's wildly successful DX7 synthesizer—released in 1983 to become one of the earliest and best-selling digital synthesizers in history. Even Miku's blue-green hair was meant to match the indicator light on the DX7 control panel (Shiba 2014). For Ito, embedding DTM components in the character's image aimed at "a science fiction-like design where human and electronic parts become one" (Shiba 2014: 41 my translation).

3.5.2 Introducing Future's First Voice Donors

3.5.2.1 Zero-G's Lola, Leon, and Miriam
Perhaps the most mysterious aspect of Yamaha's singing synthesis technology is that an ineffable quality of the original singer's voice seems to remain in the synthesized output. The session singers recorded databases in a week of five-hour sessions for Lola and Leon, the first two Vocaloid products, which were designed and released by British media company Zero-G (Werde 2003). The voice donors for the Lola and Leon Virtual Soul Vocalist fonts were Jamaican and Black British (Eidsheim 2018), and

they brought something of their particular dialects' pronunciations to recording sessions. This aspect of each voice font remained noticeable to fans, even after the Vocaloid engine's concatenative synthesis and users' adjustments in pitch, timing, inflection, vibrato, tone color, and phrasing enabled by the software controls—perhaps highlighted in part by the mismatch between the African American roots of the soul genre and the singers' native British and Caribbean dialects of English.

Unlike the unattributed Black vocalists who provided the inaugural Vocaloid products, the data for Zero-G's third product, the Miriam font, was provided by a singer named Miriam Stockley (Werde 2003). Initially "horrified" at the prospect, Stockley decided to relinquish control of her vocal likeness to Vocaloid, observing, "you can't fight progress, no matter how strange it sounds" (Stockley qtd. in Werde 2003). Stockley received a percentage of sales, in exchange for permission for the Miriam font to be marketed as a backup singer and used as an instrument legally distinct from Stockley herself (Werde 2003). Even as it was still impossible for users to "make their own fonts" since the technology required "deep knowledge of phonetics and audio engineering ... and a database of thousands of articulations," a Zero-G spokesperson mused upon future "vocal reanimation" of famous singers such as Elvis Presley as well as "computer-produced music" created through data analysis and algorithmic composition: "Start with any number of existing programs that randomly generate music. Run those files through Hit Song Science, the software that has analyzed 3.5 million songs to determine mathematic patterns in hit music. ... Throw in a lyric-generating program, several of which can be found free online, and then route the notes and lyrics through Vocaloid to give the song a voice" (Werde 2003).

3.5.2.2 Crypton Future Media's Hatsune Miku: Fujita Saki
In its design of Character Vocal Series products for Vocaloid 2 in 2007, Crypton Future Media did not hide the identities of voice donors. The database for Hatsune Miku, the first of Crypton Future Media's Character Vocals, was provided by voice actor Fujita Saki, known by fans as Sakkii (Fujita 2013). As Miku and the Character Vocals skyrocketed in popularity, Fujita herself became part of the publicity. The 2013 *Mikupedia*, a collectible publication, includes a multi-page spread featuring Fujita on site visits to several companies "cheering on" [*ōen shiteru*] Miku by marketing character goods from games to snacks to bespoke figures and original illustrations (*Hatsune* 2013). As cultural critic Ishida Maki observes:

"Vocaloid has not completely lost its body. No matter how much of the voice library has been converted into data, Hatsune Miku has not completely lost the physical relationship with the body of the voice actor Fujita Saki, who provided the voice. What is lost in the Vocaloid is not the body itself, but only its form" (Ishida 2008: 89 my translation).

Reminiscent of Miku's bio, Fujita's birth date, height, and hobbies are listed along with her other well-known voice roles; a giveaway of limited edition prints of a Hatsune Miku illustration signed by Fujita (rather than KEI, the avatar's original illustrator) is also advertised (*Hatsune* 2013: 78). Fujita herself states about her work on Miku:

> What makes me happiest about having played the role of Miku is that I could meet many different people because of her. There are many people in the world trying to express something together with Miku, not only through illustrations and music; she brings together people with many different talents. I am grateful to have been blessed with the opportunity to be by her side as she grows with the power of all these people. (Fujita 2013: 61 my translation)

Perhaps the longstanding popularity of anime and the prevalence of voice acting (*naka no hito*, lit. "inside person") as a career account not only for Fujita's apparent ease with being "in charge" (*tantō*) of the voice of an animated singing character but also what facilitated the rise of the Character Vocals phenomenon that fueled the rapid improvements of Yamaha's singing synthesis technology—ultimately presaging today's AI singing synthesis, which uses machine learning based on the audio input of humans—while actually synthesizing the voices using the data provided by the voice recordings.

References

Aitken, Jim. 2004. Zero-G Vocaloid Miriam—Vocal Synthesis Software (PC). *Keyboard*. September 1, 76.

Azad, Kalid. 2017. An Interactive Guide to The Fourier Transform. *Better Explained*. Website. Accessed 11 November 2024. https://betterexplained.com/articles/an-interactive-guide-to-the-fourier-transform/

Beller, Grégory, Diemo Schwarz, Thomas Hueber, and Xavier Rodet. 2005. A Hybrid Concatenative Synthesis System on the Intersection of Music and Speech. *Journées d'Informatique Musicale* 12:41–45.

Bennett, Gerald, and Xavier Rodet. 1989. Synthesis of the Singing Voice. In *Current Directions in Computer Music*, ed. Max V. Mathews and John Pierce, 20–44. Cambridge, MA: MIT Press.

"Bicycle Built for Two." 1962. *Music from Mathematics: Played by IBM 7090 Computer and Digital to Sound Transducer*. LP. New York: Decca (DL9103).

Bonada, Jordi, and Alex Loscos. 2003. Sample-based Singing Voice Synthesizer by Spectral Concatenation. In *Proceedings of the Stockholm Music Acoustic Conference, Stockholm, Sweden*.

Bonada, Jordi, Òscar Celma, Àlex Loscos, Jaume Ortolà, Xavier Serra, Yasuo Yoshioka, Hiraku Kayama, Yuji Hisaminato, and Hideki Kenmochi. 2001. Singing Voice Synthesis Combining Excitation Plus Resonance and Sinusoidal plus Residual Models. In *International Computer Music Conference Proceedings, Havana, Cuba*.

Chan, Paul. 2020. *The Psychoacoustics and Synthesis of Singing Harmony*. Doctoral Thesis. Nanyang Technological University, Singapore. School of Computer Science and Engineering.

Clarke, Arthur. 1998. Foreword: The Birth of HAL. In *HAL's Legacy: 2001's Computer as Dream and Reality*, ed. David G. Stork, xi–xvi. Cambridge, MA: MIT Press.

Conner, Thomas. 2013. *Rei Toei Lives! Hatsune Miku and the Design of the Virtual Pop Star*. Master's Thesis. University of Illinois, Chicago. Department of Communication.

Cook, Perry. 1993. SPASM, a Real-Time Vocal Tract Physical Model Controller; and Singer, the Companion Software Synthesis System. *Computer Music Journal* 17 (1): 30–44.

Cook, Perry. 1996. Singing Voice Synthesis: History, Current Work, and Future Directions. *Computer Music Journal* 20 (3): 38–46.

Dacre, Harry. 1892. "Daisy Bell (Bicycle Built for Two)." Song. T.B. Harms & Co. In *Johns Hopkins University Levy Sheet Music Collection, Box 140, Item 090*. Accessed 12 March 2025. http://jhir.library.jhu.edu/handle/1774.2/21250

Eidsheim, Nina Sun. 2018. *The Race of Sound: Listening, Timbre and Vocality in African American Music*. Durham: Duke University Press.

Fourier, Jean Baptiste Joseph. 2008. In *Complete Dictionary of Scientific Biography*, Vol. 5, 93–99. Detroit, MI: Charles Scribner's Sons.

Fourier's Transformational Thinking. 2018. *Nature* 555:413. https://doi.org/10.1038/d41586-018-03389-w

Fujita, Saki. 2013. Seiyū Fujita Saki no Mikumiku Gaisha Hōmon ['Mikimiku' Company Visits with Voice Actor Saki Fujita.] Interview. *Hatsune Miku Kōshiki Gaidobukku Mikupedia*. Tokyo: Magazine House Mook, 60–71.

Hamasaki, Masahiro, Hideaki Takeda, Tom Hope, and Takuichi Nishimura. 2009. Network Analysis of an Emergent Massively Collaborative Creation Community: How Can People Create Videos Collaboratively without Collaboration?

Proceedings of the International AAAI Conference on Web and Social Media 3(1): 222–225. Accessed 14 October 2014. https://doi.org/10.1609/icwsm.v3i1.14000

Hatsune Miku Kōshiki Gaidobukku Mikupedia [Mikupedia, the Official Guide to Hatsune Miku]. 2013. Tokyo: Magazine House Mook.

Hernández, Álvaro David. 2020. Hatsune Miku and the Double Nature of Voice Library Software: Content Consumption and Production in Japan. *Dōjin Journal* 1, 37–47.

Hiller, Lejaren, and Leonard Isaacson. 1959. *Experimental Music: Composition with an Electronic Computer*. New York: McGraw-Hill.

Immink, Kees. 1998. The Compact Disc Story. *Journal of the Audio Engineering Society* 46 (5): 458–465.

Ishida, Miki. 2008. "Naka no Hito" ni Naru: Koemodoki ga Kanō ni Shita Mono [Becoming a Voice Actor/Person Inside: What Voice Imitation Has Made Possible.]. *Eureka: Shi to Sōtokushū: Hatsune Miku Netto ni Maifurita Tenshi* 40 (15): 88–94.

Kenmochi, Hideki. 2010. VOCALOID and Hatsune Miku Phenomenon in Japan. *InterSinging 2010: First Interdisciplinary Workshop on Singing Voice Conference Proceedings*. Accessed 19 May 2014. www.isca-speech.org/archive/int_singing_2010/papers/isi0_001.pdf

Kenmochi, Hideki. 2012. Singing Synthesis as a New Musical Instrument. In *IEEE Conference Proceedings*, 5385–5388.

Kenmochi, Hideki, and Ken Fujimoto. 2014. *Bōkaroido Gijutsuron: Utagoe Gōsei no Kiso to Sono Shikumi* [Vocaloid Technology: Basic Singing Voice Synthesis and Its Structure]. Tokyo: Yamaha Music Media.

Kurita, Kaori. 2014. *Tomita Isao: Koko Kara Saki e* [Isao Tomita: From Here on Out] Poketto Miku Kōshiki Bukku. Tokyo: Gakken Educational Publishing, 18–21.

Logic System. 2003. Ano Subarashii Ai wo Mō Ichido [That Wonderful Love, Once More.] *History of Logic System*. CD. EMI Japan: TOCT-25079.

Loscos, Àlex. 2019. YAMAHA, Aishiteru Totemo Aishiteru Hontoni [Yamaha, We Love You So Much, We Really Love You]. *BMAT Music Innovators*. Blog Post. Accessed 26 March 2025. https://www.bmat.com/bmat-yamaha-music-technologies/

Macon, Michael, Leslie Jensen-Link, James Oliviero, Mark Clements, and E. Bryan George. 1997. Concatenation-based MIDI-to Singing Voice Synthesis. *Journal of Audio Engineering Society* 45 (9): 1–10.

New Developed AI Synthesis Engine Produces Natural, Richly Expressive Vocals. 2022. *Yamaha: Make Waves*. Website. https://www.yamaha.com/en/news_release/2022/22101301/ Accessed 1 December 2023.

Park, Tae Hong. 2009. An Interview with Max Mathews. *Computer Music Journal* 33 (3): 9–22.

Pickett, J. M. 1999. *The Acoustics of Speech Communication: Fundamentals, Speech Perception Theory, and Technology.* Needham Heights, MA: Allyn & Bacon.

Puckette, Miller. 2020. The Contributions of Charles Dodge's Speech Songs to Computer Music Practice. In *Between the Tracks: Musicians on Selected Electronic Music*, ed. Miller Puckette and Kerry Hagan, 63–82. Cambridge, MA: MIT Press.

Roads, Curtis. 1980. Interview with Max Mathews. *Computer Music Journal* 4 (4): 15–22.

Rodet, Xavier. 2002. Synthesis and Processing of the Singing Voice. In *Proceedings of the 1st IEEE Benelux Workshop on Model based [sic] Processing and Coding of Audio, Leuven, Belgium.*

Rodet, Xavier, Yves Potard, and Jean-Baptiste Barrière. 1984. The CHANT Project: From the Synthesis of the Singing Voice to Synthesis in General. *Computer Music Journal* 8 (3): 15–31.

Schwarz, Diemo. 2005. Current Research in Concatenative Sound Synthesis. In *Proceedings of the International Computer Music Conference (ICMC), Barcelona, Spain.*

Schwarz, Diemo. 2006. Concatenative Sound Synthesis: The Early Years. *Journal of New Music Research* 35 (1): 3–22.

Schwarz, Diemo. 2007. Corpus-Based Concatenative Synthesis. *IEEE Signal Processing Magazine* 24 (2), 92–104.

Schwarz, Diemo, Gregory Beller, Bruno Verbrugghe, and Sam Britton. 2006. Real-time Corpus-based Concatenative Synthesis with CataRT. *9th International Conference on Digital Audio Effects (DAFx-06) Montreal.* Conference Proceedings: DAFX1-DAFX7.

Serra, Xavier, and Julius Smith. 1990. Spectral Modeling Synthesis: A Sound Analysis/Synthesis System Based on a Deterministic plus Stochastic Decomposition. *Computer Music Journal* 14 (4): 12–24.

Shiba, Tomonori. 2014. *Hatsune Miku wa Naze Sekai o Kaeta no ka?* [Why Did Hatsune Miku Change the World?] Tokyo: Ōta Shuppan.

Smith, Julius. 2007. *Mathematics of the Discrete Fourier Transform (DFT), with Audio Applications.* Website. Accessed 1 November 2024. https://ccrma.stanford.edu/~jos/mdft/

Smith, Julius. 2010. *Physical Audio Signal Processing for Virtual Musical Instruments and Digital Audio Effects.* Stanford: W3K Publishing.

Smith, Julius. 2011. *Spectral Audio Signal Processing.* Stanford: W3K Publishing.

St. Michel, Patrick. 2014. The Making of Vocaloid. *Red Bull Music Academy.* Website. Accessed 3 April 2016. http://daily.redbullmusicacademy.com/2014/11/vocaloid-feature

Takahashi, Nobuyuki (Studio Hard Deluxe). 2011. *Bōkaroido Genshō: Shinseiki Kontentsu Sangyō no Mirai Moderu* [Vocaloid Phenomenon: A Future Model for the Content Industry in the New Century]. Tokyo: PHP Institute.

Walden, John. 2004. Yamaha Vocaloid Leon & Lola. *Sound on Sound*. Accessed 14 March 2018. https://www.soundonsound.com/reviews/yamaha-vocaloid-leon-lola

Werde, Bill. 2003. Could I Get That Song in Elvis, Please? 2003. *New York Times*, November 23: AR1.

Yamaha Vocaloid. 2003. Voice Synthesis that Doesn't Sound Like a Robot. *Popular Science* 262(6): 91.

Young, Kar Fai Samson. 2013. A "Digital Opera" at the Boundaries of Transnationalism: The Synthesized Voices in Zuni Icosahedron's The Memory Palace of Matteo Ricci. In *Vocal Music and Cultural Identity in Contemporary Music: Unlimited Voices in East Asia and the West*, ed. Christian Utz and Frederick Lau, 203–224. New York: Routledge.

CHAPTER 4

Future Voices to Come: AI Singing After Miku

Abstract This chapter opens with an account of Vocaloid's 2019 premier of the AI Hibari voicebank, which was trained on the archive of a renowned twentieth-century Japanese singer. The chapter then offers an overview of artificial intelligence followed by an exploration of the current impact of machine learning on singing voice synthesis (SVS). A discussion of the history and scope of the field of AI covers key technical distinctions, such as predictive versus generative AI and supervised versus unsupervised algorithms. The chapter also introduces deep neural networks (DNN), natural language processing (NLP), and large language models (LLM), while touching on the roles and significance of foundation models and transformer architectures. The chapter compares how different singing voice synthesis systems approach AI training. Several DNN-based SVS systems are presented, including VOCALOID:AI, demonstrated in 2019 with AI Hibari and released for sale in 2022 as Vocaloid 6 with Vocalo Changer, a vocal timbre transfer tool. Concerns surrounding voice cloning are examined through case studies from East Asia between 2018 and 2022. The issue of deepfakes in the USA and Europe is then examined, focusing on the study of Holly Herndon's Holly+ and Spawning in comparison with Grimes' Elf.tech. A brief survey of current singing voice synthesis products is undertaken. The chapter concludes with consideration of how to approach ethical concerns about artificial intelligence in singing synthesis.

© The Author(s), under exclusive license to Springer Nature Switzerland AG 2025
G. Jude, *How Vocaloid Works*,
https://doi.org/10.1007/978-3-031-92727-0_4

Keywords AI Hibari • DNN singing voice synthesis (2016–2025) • Deepfakes • Voice clones • Vocal timbre transfer • Holly+ • Holly Herndon's Spawning • Grimes' Elf.tech • Vocalo Change • Ado (Japanese singer)

4.1 Yamaha's Debut of VOCALOID:AI: Making a New "Old Song"

On September 29, 2019, NHK (Japan Broadcasting Corporation) featured a special program, "Bringing Misora Hibari Back with AI," about a new song in old-fashioned *enka* style, "Arekara" [Ever Since Then] (Arekara—NHK 2019; Tanii 2019a). This was the debut of Yamaha's AI Hibari voicebank and its VOCALOID:AI, 'performed' by a holographic rendering of the voicebank's long-deceased donor, Shōwa-Era superstar Misora Hibari (Grace 2019). Leaving behind Vocaloid's characteristic futuristic pop vision, AI Hibari appealed to the nostalgia evoked by the (still-popular) post-war enka genre, which flamboyantly expresses longing for rural hometown life and a traditional Japanese essence (Yano 2002). The song, produced by lyricist and Misora Hibari collaborator Akimoto Yasushi (with music composed by winner of the project's public submission process Satō Kafū), takes the perspective of the deceased singer herself, "looking back" on happy times while "watching over" her listening fans (Burnt and Kasai 2024: 418). Backed by lushly produced piano and orchestra, AI Hibari sings with the original enka singer's trademark wide *yuri* vibrato and rich timbre, clearly evoking Misora Hibari's vocal presence and expressivity. Yet the AI's lack of guttural depth in the lower notes and the predictable evenness of the vibrato seem to tone down the embodied emotionality of Misora Hibari—the artist dubbed "queen of tears" by music scholar Christine Yano (Yano 2002: 121). Interestingly, AI Hibari also bears sonic resemblance to her predecessor Hatsune Miku in the glides between notes, the slightly mushy consonants, and particularly the recurrent metallic sheen (particularly on sung vowels 'ah' and 'ee'). AI Hibari seems designed to broaden Vocaloid's audience beyond the demographic first captured by Hatsune Miku in the 2010s.

4.2 Artificial Intelligence: From Robots to Generative AI

4.2.1 What Is Artificial Intelligence? How Machines Learn (to Sing)

The term 'artificial intelligence' dates back to 1955, when mathematician John McCarthy began organizing a conference about the potential of thinking machines. The Dartmouth Summer Research Project on Artificial Intelligence, which included Claude Shannon and Marvin Minsky, is considered the foundational event in the field (Frana 2021). The dream (or nightmare) of an intelligent human-made agent goes back further, imagined by science fiction authors such as Karel Čapek, the early twentieth-century Czech writer who coined the term 'robot,' and American novelist of Russian Jewish birth Isaac Asimov, who formulated an ethical system to protect humans from their creations: the three laws of robotics[1] laid out in the early 1940s during the development of his influential Foundation series. British computer scientist Alan Turing suggested conversational behavior as a means of telling a human from a computer, Turing test (Russell and Norvig 2021).

While the notion of humanoid robots roaming freely might sound alarming (or appealing), the reality of AI is far from the dystopian vision of *The Terminator* world of Skynet. Artificial intelligence does not equate to sentience, consciousness, or human-like will. Broadly construed, artificial intelligence refers to any computer system that simulates "human learning, comprehension, problem solving, decision making, creativity and autonomy" (Stryker and Kavla 2024). Narayanan and Kapoor (2024) offer an even broader definition, describing AI as "an umbrella term for a set of loosely related technologies" (1). Russell and Norvig (2021) highlight the lack of consensus on the definition of intelligence itself, noting that most AI researchers prioritize a practical, task-oriented approach to the field (Russell and Norvig 2021). Accordingly, a successful machine learning algorithm is said to "learn" when its performance improves by processing more data relevant to the tasks it is designed for (Goodfellow et al. 2016: 97).

Narayanan and Kapoor suggest three criteria are hallmarks of AI today: (1) if the task requires creative input or feedback from a human, (2)

---

[1] In "Runaround," a short story included in Asimov's 1950 collection *I, Robot*.

whether the behavior emerges indirectly rather than being directed by code, and (3) whether the system behaves autonomously, demonstrating adaptability (Narayanan and Kapoor 2024: 12–13). Artificial intelligence can currently be roughly divided into predictive and generative AI, with many types still falling outside these categories (Narayanan and Kapoor 2024: 10).

Statistical algorithms have been used by computer scientists for decades prior to the development of machine learning to recognize patterns in datasets in order to perform specific tasks by induction (without explicit instructions from a programmer). Mathematical models that are trained on data to adjust their parameters in order to minimize prediction errors are considered part of machine learning systems. There are many such algorithms with useful applications: for instance, linear regression analysis predicts values based on other values, making it useful in assessing financial trends and risks, while logistic regression, an algorithm used to calculate the probability of an event, can be employed to predict an outbreak of disease within a community (Stryker and Kavla 2024).

Both linear and logical regression are examples of supervised learning algorithms, meaning they require human labeling of data sets during training. Supervised machine learning occurs through observing the human mapping of relations between input and output (Russell and Norvig 2021). In contrast, unsupervised machine learning is designed to "discover hidden patterns of data groupings" on its own (Stryker and Kavla 2024). This approach allows multiple layers of algorithms to run automatically, simulating human cognitive functions to "extract meaning and relationships from large volumes of unstructured, unlabeled data" (Stryker and Kavla 2024). Increasingly, 'deep' learning models, so called because of this layering, are used to generate original content modeled on input datasets.

4.2.2 *Generative AI: From Language to Audio*

After decades of growth and setbacks in the broader field of artificial intelligence, generative AI (sometimes called gen AI) has recently exploded into public consciousness. Generative AI, which produces original digital output closely resembling human creativity, can be traced back to models of synaptic connections in the human brain developed in the mid-twentieth century (Narayanan and Kapoor 2024: 105)—leading to the term neural networks. In the early twenty-first century, the emergence of massive and complex datasets dubbed "big data," coupled with more powerful computing resources that enabled the processing and analysis of these datasets, fueled innovation (Russell and Norvig 2021). Natural Language Processing (NLP) utilizes algorithms based on rule-based and statistical models, as well as newer deep learning models, to understand and generate human language (Stryker and Holdsworth 2024). NLP has been applied to tasks such as machine translation, auto-correction, and chatbots (Russell and Norvig 2021), with Apple's Siri, introduced in 2011, successfully combining speech recognition and voice-commands to assist human users in simple verbal tasks. Large language models (LLMs), which gained widespread attention in late 2022 with the release of ChatGPT, rely on deep neural network architectures to generate convincingly human-like text (Stryker and Holdsworth 2024).

Deep neural networks (DNN) incorporate multiple layers of computational circuits called neurons, placed between the model's input and output layers. This layered structure creates longer computation paths, enabling more complex interaction among input variables (Goodfellow et al. 2016: 750–751). An optimization algorithm called backpropagation (short for backward propagation of error) is essential to the training of deep learning models. It calculates the adjustments to the network's internal settings, called weights, needed to minimize error or loss and improve the model's performance (Bergman and Stryker 2024). DNNs are currently the most effective at perception tasks (Narayanan and Kapoor 2024: 114) and are thus fundamental in systems that generate images, video, and audio content. NLP deep neural networks such as WaveNet are also providing increasingly natural-sounding text-to-speech synthesis (Russell and Norvig 2021).

Generative AI using deep neural networks starts with a foundation model, which is trained on massive amounts of raw data. The foundation model is then adapted to specific tasks through a process called fine-tuning, which may involve either supervised learning (requiring a labeled dataset) or reinforcement learning with human feedback (RLHF). Output generated by the AI is then assessed by users for further refinement, while the foundational model is updated less frequently (Stryker and Kavla 2024).

Since 2017, generative AI models have shifted to using transformer architectures, which handle input data more efficiently by using parallel processing rather than sequential processing (Stryker and Kavla 2024). Transformers have significantly improved speed and scalability of AI systems (Merritt 2022). These innovations account for why the output of gen AI is increasingly capable of producing content—whether text, audio, image, or video—that is indistinguishable from work created by humans.

4.3 Approaches to DNN Singing Voice Synthesis (SVS): From WaveNet to DeepSinger

4.3.1 Transition from Older Synthesis Models

Research on singing voice synthesis published in the mid-2010s marked a shift, from previous approaches, such as concatenative synthesis, to machine learning-based models. In 2016, researchers at Nagoya Institute of Technology found that a DNN-based singing synthesis framework was ranked as more natural-sounding by ten Japanese listeners compared to another SVS model[2] (Nishimura et al. 2016). The following year, former Vocaloid development team member Jordi Bonada, along with Merlijn Blaauw, presented a singing synthesizer model based on WaveNet, a deep neural network developed for text-to-speech synthesis through generation of raw audio (Blaauw and Bonada 2017). While no demonstration audio accompanies their publication, Blaauw and Bonada's modification of the WaveNet network architecture to include musical features such as pitch, timbre, and timing promised to effectively bridge the distinction between speech and singing synthesis (Blaauw and Bonada 2017).

4.3.2 Sinsy: Database Training and Score Reading

Sinsy, a SVS service launched online in 2009 by a research team at Nagoya Institute of Technology, integrated neural networks into its publicly available system in 2018 (Hono et al. 2018). Similar to Yamaha's Vocaloid, Sinsy's synthesized voices are modeled on voicebanks provided by individual human singers—as of 2018, Japanese, English,[3] and Mandarin Chinese voice synthesis options are available (Hono et al. 2018). Sinsy reads a musical score uploaded by the user, converting the notated score and lyrics into audio. Short samples provided online indicate variable results; sample f00005j most resembles a recording of human

---

[2] An important statistical modeling technique called the hidden Markov model (HMM).
[3] Several English voicebanks have distinctly Japanese accents, indicating training on input by native Japanese speaking vocalists.

vocalization—or perhaps sounds closest to Vocaloid, which my ears are accustomed to hearing as 'good' singing synthesis (Sinsy 2024). In addition to training their neural network to provide a smooth flow of on-pitch, convincingly human-like vocals, the developers prioritize user control of vibrato level, which is challenging since vibrato is not typically notated in a musical score (Hono et al. 2018).

4.3.3 Training a Deep Neural Network: Spawn and Holly+

Released in May 2019, Holly Herndon's album *PROTO* features AI-generated vocals reflecting Herndon's aesthetic aim and effect. Herndon, a Berlin-based singer-songwriter, led a collaborative effort with husband Mat Dryhurst, developer Jules LaPlace, and an ensemble of singers to design and train a DIY deep neural network called Spawn (Stubbs 2019). The resulting album embraces Spawn's glitchy weirdness, with songs showcasing hybridization of eclectic styles and genres. "Eternal," with its dramatic beat and backing chorus of bright female vocals, released as an official video featuring multiple singers along with Herndon herself, all digitally blended and visually jittering. The song features Herndon's/Spawn's harmonized soprano line, dramatized by reverb and impossibly high notes that resemble purposeful overuse of AutoTune pitch correction. The main melody line has a tendency toward metallic brightness (particularly in the breaths) which resembles Vocaloid synthesis—whether due to my careful aural attention or my grasping at words to explain what I am hearing, I remain uncertain. Listening to this rich and complex palette of sounds woven into a masterfully structured pop song, it is unclear which vocal sounds originate from which source. While the melody is timbrally Herndon's voice, on *PROTO*, the distinction between human and synthesized singing is purposefully blurred if not rendered entirely irrelevant (Holly Herndon—Eternal 2019).

Both Holly Herndon's Spawn and Yamaha's AI Hibari, released later in the same year (Yamaha VOCALOID 2019), utilize deep neural networks trained on custom datasets. As the sounds synthesized by digital technology become increasingly similar to the sounds of human singing, the aesthetic preferences of the creator and the subjective experiences of the listener come into sharper focus. In a promotional video, Herndon documents the process of training Spawn, starting with the creation of an output model based on her own voice. This AI model required Herndon to provide "a canon of audio material" consisting of phrases both spoken and sung. Herndon, who completed a Ph.D. at Stanford's Center for Computer Research in Music and Acoustics (CCRMA), also trained "baby" Spawn on fifteen singers' voices in addition to her own. Participants spent hours of "learning sessions" in Herndon's studio, vocalizing solo and together, as well as listening to Spawn's responses to their input in real time (Holly Herndon Shares 2019). This allowed the team to "sift through and find the best bits," changing their approach as necessary and trying different types of input during the recursive training process (Holly Herndon Shares 2019). Herndon notes the surprisingly low-fidelity results, which she describes as "raspy textural sound" which she links audibly to early sound recordings[4] (Holly Herndon Shares 2019).

4.3.4 Training by Archive: AI Hibari

Yamaha's AI Hibari was trained on the deceased singer's recording archive, controlled by Nippon Columbia recording label. In creating this model, the VOCALOID:AI team also had access to two hours' worth of bedtime stories read and recorded onto cassette tapes by Hibari for her son, who donated this personal material to the project (Tanii 2019b). The archive provided to Yamaha included about 1500 songs recorded over the course of Misora Hibari's decades-long career, on various analog and digital media formats (Tanii 2019a, b). This presented the VOCALOID:AI team with two major challenges. First, how could the AI system be designed to deal with the variations of Hibari's vocal tone quality and singing style not only in different genres but also over her lifetime as an artist? Second, how could they devise a machine learning set-up that could distinguish between the sounds of different recording media and studio conditions? In short, VOCALOID:AI had to be trained to recognize and mark various attributes of the voice recording data (Tanii 2019a, b). Training the system with all the recordings together resulted in "a thick-sounding, hoarse, croaky voice" (Tanii 2019a my translation). On the other hand, limiting the dataset too drastically also led to a decrease in quality, with a lack of subtlety and balance in singing style controls producing what the researchers described as "unprofessional," "uncomfortable," and even "distressed"

---

[4] The documentary short includes a demonstration of Herndon speaking into the AI system with Spawn mimicking the input in real time, then cuts to archival footage of Édouard-Léon Scott de Martinville's 1860 "First-ever recording" (Holly Herndon Shares 2019).

sounds (Tanii 2019b my translation)—perhaps not too different from the "raspy textural" output that Herndon accepted and even relished.

Rather than relying solely on audio input for training as Herndon's team did, Yamaha's project, represented by Ryūnosuke Omichi (specialist in singing voice synthesis) and Keijiro Saino (specialist in speaking voice synthesis), combined multiple DNN models to handle different aspects of the overall singing voice synthesis (Tanii 2019a, b). One model reads the musical notation of the song, while others determine features such as pitch and timing of articulation; different neural networks control the combination of these features and synthesize the final audio waveform (Tanii 2019a). The Yamaha research team gauged the results by how closely AI Hibari's rendering of "Arekara" resembled the vocal performance of the human artist herself. This aesthetic goal was judged first by a process of trial and error based on feedback from those well-versed in her singing, then later evaluated by Twitter users following the song's broadcasts. While some found the voice quality mechanical and synthetic, other fans were convinced, even moved to tears. Some found the resemblance of the synthesized voice to the deceased artist uncanny, like "a technological séance" (Tanii 2019b my translation).

4.3.5 *Training by Extraction: DeepSinger*

In contrast to the unique datasets used for intensive training by Herndon and Yamaha (as well as the Sinsy team to some extent), a Zhejiang University research team led by Yi Ren and Xu Tan prioritized efficiency in their SVS system, DeepSinger (Ren et al. 2020a). First, the developers collected tens of thousands of songs and lyrics in three languages from an unspecified music website, thus bypassing the need to record human singing data (Ren et al. 2020a). They combined their singing model (based on the FastSpeech text-to-speech model) with an alignment model, which helps align audio signals with textual representations, thus circumventing the human effort required to match singing with lyrics and label durations of sung phonemes (Ren et al. 2020a: 1981). Thus, their dataset, Singing-Wild, which spans 92 hours and includes 89 different singers, enables the synthesis of singing in Mandarin, Cantonese, and English while eliminating human data labeling and model training. Finally, the singing model architecture of DeepSinger, which includes lyrics, pitch, and reference encoders along with a decoder, incorporates transformer blocks that enhance the system's efficiency by enabling parallel processing (Ren et al. 2020a).

Listening to the extremely short (between one and six seconds) audio demos provided on the group's website (Ren et al. 2020b), I hear synthesized vocal timbres distinct from the subtle metallic quality of Spawn and AI Hibari—instead, a glitchy, cascading warble that creates a unique lo-fi digital effect, reminiscent of an old love song downloaded, copied, and recopied to share. Given the team's goal of "generating beautiful AI singing voices with unique styles which can bring new artistic experiences," DeepSinger can be considered a success in this regard (Ren et al. 2020a: 1987). On the other hand, the large-scale collection of songs and voices from the Internet hints at some of the wider issues at stake as AI takes center stage in the realm of singing synthesis.

4.4 Managing AI Voices: Vocaloid 6, Holly+, and Elf.tech

4.4.1 From Voice Clones to Vocalo Changer: AI in Asia 2018–2022

In December 2018, Chinese idol girl group SNH48 (an offshoot of Japan's iconic AKB48, cf. Xie 2021) released a music video debuting the group members' "digital clones," a demonstration by California-based AI company ObEN of its personal artificial intelligence (PAI) system (ObEN 2018). According to ObEN, each performer's digital avatar was generated from a database of 100–200 recorded sentences (Datta 2019). In the music video, "Now and Forever," conventional pop audio production, including processing of vocals, renders the idols' singing indistinguishable from their clones,' while the visual avatars are not only obviously animated but also doll-sized onscreen perhaps to avoid the uncanny valley effect. The quality of the virtual stars' vocal performances aside, the economic benefits to the entertainment industry are clearly articulated: virtual versions of popular stars are eternally youthful and completely controllable, while providing immersive, interactive, and intimate modes of fan engagement via mobile devices (Jing 2018; ObEN 2018). ObEN's CEO states, "PAI provides SNH48's audience with new types of content—one that blends man and machine into a unique entertainment experience" (Jain qtd. in ObEN 2018). The case of the SNH48 digital clones heralds the broad potential applications of AI singing synthesis. For instance, in 2022, Chinese tech firm Tencent Music Entertainment claimed to have used its Lingyin Engine to produce over 1000 AI-voiced songs, including "the first song by an AI singer to be streamed over 100 million times across the internet" (Stassen 2022).

Yamaha's AI Hibari performance on NHK indicates that consideration of a technology's use and reception is clearly crucial. The lukewarm response to Yamaha's showcasing of VOCALOID:AI was at least partly due to miscalculations of audience reactions to the wider context, rather than a failure of the technology itself. The virtual performance, which included a detailed holographic projection of the artist, struck some fans as "'profaning the dead'" (Brunt and Kasai 2024: 418). Furthermore, the new song's lyrics, from the first-person perspective of Hibari herself, were viewed as "speaking through [her] voice without [her] consent" (Brunt and Kasai 2024: 418). In addition, AI Hibari may have seemed unimpressive as an attempt at providing autonomous, responsive AI technology (Brunt and Kasai 2024: 419). Repetition of the single official song "may have led to this case often being equated with a pre-prepared recording" rather than demonstrating a groundbreaking advancement in the software that enables a new level of original creation (Brunt and Kasai 2024: 419).

The virtual appearance of AI Hibari on NHK was also controversial since the singer herself had refused to appear on the network later in her life. As Zaborowski writes: "To have her appear posthumously on the flagship NHK show was a slap in the face to fans who considered the Hibari-NHK feud canon—and the performance was deemed disrespectful to Hibari's 'true' persona" (Zaborowski 2025: 226). While AI Hibari was featured at Tokyo's Mori Art Museum from December 2019 until the end of February 2020, with explanations of both the singing synthesis system and the 3D video rendering of the song (Exhibition-Related 2019), it is clear that the release of AI Hibari on NHK cooled fan reception of Yamaha's groundbreaking product—which also unfortunately intersected with the start of the global COVID-19 pandemic. The power of audience reception underlines the efficacy of the conceptual and marketing design of character voices like Hatsune Miku, which provide users with an image for the synthesized singer that is flexible enough to allow creation of a variety of works with the product within what Zaborowski calls the "fanon," a neologism combining "fan" and "canon" (Zaborowski 2025: 222).

A similar dilemma arose in South Korea in late 2020 and early 2021, when AI startup Supertone created AI voice clones of Korean singers for *Competition of the Century: AI vs Human*, a TV variety show aired on the national broadcast channel SBS (Bae 2021). The appearance on the show of a voice model of beloved 1990s music star Kim Kwang Seok, who passed away at age 31 in 1996, ignited controversy that sparked discussion of AI ethics (Artificial Intelligence 2021). However, Supertone's promises to voice clone K-pop supergroup BTS spurred a massive influx of investment into the company (Stassen 2021).

In October 2022, Yamaha finally released its new product, Vocaloid 6 bundled with VOCALOID:AI and the Vocalo Changer plugin (New Developed AI 2022). The selling point of Vocaloid's Version 6, as demonstrated on Yamaha's website, is that a user can transform their own singing; audio input (in Japanese or English) is converted into the timbre of any of the AI voicebanks (of either gender), then made available for audio composition in the Vocaloid workflow (New Developed AI 2022). Yamaha's newest SVS software, released three years after the AI Hibari debut of VOCALOID:AI—four years after Vocaloid's previous version—gives users a chameleon-like power to manipulate their own voices far beyond the well-used (and famously repurposed) pitch correction software, AutoTune, of the late 1990s.

Voice synthesis also currently sidesteps potential legal issues that may arise from either utilizing "distinctive celebrity voices" or imitating the voice of an ordinary citizen for fraudulent purposes (Ando 2024: 171). As Toyo University professor of law Kazuhiro Ando points out, vocal synthesis technology complicated copyright issues; but since concatenative synthesis uses a method that "extracts" vocal features from a large database, the resulting synthesized voice is "not physically identical to the original sound" and therefore does not infringe copyright (Ando 2024: 174). Whether (or when) AI-generated digital voice clones will be legally controlled (or controllable), artists have been at the forefront of the fight to protect their own work, including the sound of their own voice.

4.4.2 Deepfakes to DAO: From Spawn to Spawning, 2019–2022

Although unauthorized computer-generated images of celebrities began circulating in the latter half of the 2010s, audio deepfakes brought the issue into the public eye. A text-to-speech model trained on Jay-Z recordings rapped a Shakespeare soliloquy in 2020. Yet the ability of vocalists to take legal action remained limited as "vocal style" is not covered under U.S. copyright and cannot be considered misappropriation, so long as the deepfake is labeled as such (Hogan 2020). Peter Martin, CEO of immersive media company VALIS Studio, claims: "Deepfake is very democratizing"; yet the issue increasingly plagues celebrities, with superstar Scarlett Johansson stating, after no less than three lawsuits involving gen AI misuse of her audio and audiovisual image between 2023 and 2025: "The threat of AI affects each and every one of us" (Scharf 2025).

Herndon's 2021 release and distribution of the Holly+ voice tool (presumably based on the own 2019 Spawn AI voice model) included legal protections of her "digital twin" (Herndon 2021). The Holly+ voice tool allows users to upload up to five minutes of original audio content and receive "a download of that music sung back in [Herndon's] distinctive processed voice" (Herndon 2021). The licensing of Herndon's vocal likeness for commercial use was handled under Decentralised Autonomous Organization (DAO) stewardship. The DAO token holders had a vote in the minting of NFTs for derivative works using Holly+. If the vote passed, the creator of a work using Holly+ would receive 50% of profits, with 40% going to the DAO members and 10% to Herndon herself.[5]

An ensemble demonstration of Holly+ shows singers providing input to the AI (AI and Music 2022). The tool can respond by singing an original line in an appropriate genre-specific style—creating a real-time, ex tempore phrase vocalized by the Holly+ AI. It can also transform a singer's vocal input (in this case sung by Herndon's husband Mat Dryhurst) into the Holly+ timbre and range, in real time. While similar to Yamaha's Vocalo Changer, Holly+ offers live interactivity, without requiring the user to manually adjust parameters like "expressiveness." Holly+ also provides unexpected glitches—as evidenced by Dryhurst's amused reactions to hearing his own vocal input transformed into Holly+ timbre and range, emerging from the loudspeakers (AI and Music 2022). In Herndon's 2022 TED talk, singer Pher demonstrates live vocal timbre transfer using Holly+. He performs a soulful song, alternating between his own voice—amplified through one microphone—and the Holly+ vocal, which features a distinctive timbre and is pitched an octave higher than his own, through the other microphone (What If 2022).

---

[5] While Zora Protocol was the basis for the auction model with funds transferred as Ethereum blockchain, deadlinks and server errors during access indicate these Holly+ features have fallen by the wayside as of 2025.

At the end of 2022, Dryhurst and Herndon, along with CEO Jordan Meyer, cofounded Spawning, an organization promoting ethical AI training and protection for digital artists as rights holders, spawning partners internationally with Hugging Face (USA) and Stability (UK). Spawning API provides tools such as "Have I Been Trained" and "Do Not Train," which allow creators greater knowledge about and control over the uses of their own digital work while helping researchers who use datasets for AI training to avoid including non-consenting data in their work (Spawning 2022; Spawning Opts Out 2023).

4.4.3   Elf.tech and the AI Vocal Avalanche: 2023–2025

In early April 2023, a TikTok user called Ghostwriter977 uploaded a new song called "Heart on My Sleeve." Using an AI vocal filter, Ghostwriter had mimicked the voices of superstar Drake and The Weeknd (Silberling 2023). Although a statement from Drake's representative, Universal Music Group, led to the quick removal of the deepfake track from most platforms, the incident highlighted artists' lack of legal protections in the face of emerging AI technologies. As Ghostwriter—still anonymous—observed, "The genie can't be put back in the bottle" (Ghostwriter qtd. in Robinson 2023).

That same month, Canadian musician Grimes invited fans to "collaborate" with using her GrimesAI voiceprint via Elf.tech (TuneCore 2023). Using the GrimesAI system, which was developed by AI development studio CreateSafe and trained on Grimes' voice, an artist can upload their own original composition to be "sung" by the GrimesAI (Pequeño 2023). Once the song is approved by Grimes, the song is sold as a co-creation by the artist and GrimesAI, with a 50–50 royalty split. Review and distribution are facilitated by digital music service TuneCore and CreateSafe, "providing artists the opportunity to engage with AI technology in an innovative, streamlined process that provides tangible value and enables consent, control and revenue splits at scale" (Grimes 2023; TuneCore 2023). Grimes' approach to her fans' collaborative input differs from Herndon's when it comes to revenue models. Whereas Holly+ is run by a governance board of token holders who approve songs created with the Holly+ voice, the GrimesAI voiceprint is co-managed within more traditional corporate structures. However, at the time of the pilot release, Grimes was unclear about the legal rights available to her if fans created songs she did not approve (Romo 2023).

From the summer of 2023, generative AI singing synthesis apps and platforms began flooding the web. Ace Studio's offer of a "professional AI singing voice generator to create studio-quality AI vocals from MIDI and lyrics" resembles Vocaloid's timeline interface within a digital audio workstation (DAW) environment, providing over 80 royalty-free AI singers in a variety of genres (from pop to opera) and languages (including English, Spanish, Chinese, and Japanese) (Ace Studio 2023). Voice-Swap promises to "easily transform your vocals to match the style of our chart-topping singers" with testimonials by popular artists such as Diplo (Voice-Swap 2023). Kits AI tempts users with the ability to "convert your voice" with voice cloning and blending, comparing its capabilities to AI speech generator ElevenLabs (Kits AI 2024). Audimee also offers royalty-free voice libraries as well as the option to "create an AI voice using 10–15 minutes of recorded vocals" (Audimee 2023). Suno AI and Udio go a step further, offering AI music generation of fully realized songs (voice and instruments) in any genre via textbox prompts (Suno AI Music 2023; Udio Beta 2023).

Grimes and Herndon were featured in 2023's TIME100 AI list, with Grimes provocatively proclaiming that she aims to "'open-source' her identity" and looks forward to a near-future "face off" with an "AI-hive-mind-collective Grimes" alternative to her human self (Grimes qtd. in Chow 2023a). Herndon is more circumspect, critiquing the music industry more broadly by pointing out that streaming platforms "are making it harder to earn a living as a musician, and are having a flattening, dulling effect on global music" (Chow 2023b). Yet she too celebrates the creative potential of gen AI, describing Spawn as a "provocation" and reveling in the freedom of relinquishing the sound of her individual voice through AI: "It was so beautiful to see myself conveyed in someone else's expression" (Herndon qtd. in Chow 2023b). The two artists remain at the forefront of AI singing technology, with Herndon making *Business Insider*'s AI Power List 2024 and Grimes receiving a TIME100 AI Impact Award in 2025 (Moses 2024; Shah 2025).

Yet despite the optimistic sense of artistic possibility, the growing flood of AI options for singing and musical synthesis continues to provoke controversy. On February 24, 2025, over one thousand prominent British musicians and composers released a "silent album" in support of the launch of the Independent Society of Musicians' "Make It Fair" campaign (Glynn 2025). The movement vehemently opposes proposed U.K. legal changes that would ease AI developers' access to creative content for dataset training (Glynn 2025). While government officials aim to foster AI innovation in Britain, artists like Paul McCartney and Kate Bush liken the proposed changes in U.K. copyright law to theft (Glynn 2025). Opponents of the "rights reservation" plan, which would allow creators to opt out of training, argue that "it is not possible for an individual writer or artist to notify thousands of different AI service providers that they do not want their content used in that way, or to monitor what has happened to their work across the whole internet" (Glynn 2025).

Herndon maintains that, if an opt-out standard were adopted by industry leaders and policymakers, it would merit cautious optimism about the possibilities for artists to participate in establishing ethical digital practices: "We are trying to build a consent layer for how data is used in AI training. ... And so far, everyone we've talked to, including people building large models, are really interested and invested in having clean data" (Herndon qtd. in Chow 2023b). However, national and regional differences in copyright law make it challenging to protect creators, given the rapid pace of AI innovations, especially with transnational flows facilitated by the Internet. The impacts on listeners, who will increasingly encounter synthesized voices that have no single, verifiable human source, remain unexplored.

4.5 The Embodied Future of Human Singing

4.5.1 Digital Design Choices: How Our Tools Shape Us

As the power of tools such as generative artificial intelligence expands, so too does the scope and reach of these tools. The rapid adoption of LLMs has forced conversations about the ethical, legal, environmental, and security risks associated with artificial intelligence (Milmo and Hern 2024; Seeking Visions 2025). The release in early 2025 of China's DeepSeek-R1 LLM promises to provide more affordable access (Gibney 2025), with generative AI being rapidly adopted within China in private and public sectors, from the auto and home appliance industries to medical and governmental services (Lo 2025). At the same time, world business and tech leaders urge the development of environmentally sustainable AI (*Coalition for Sustainable* 2025; New Coalition 2025); although AI innovations are expected to boost the global economy, the computation power and storage they require will drive a surge in energy consumption, increasing global power needs by up to 160% by 2030 (Dubey 2025).

For musicians and music fans, the realization of the long-held dream of synthesized voice holds both promise and peril. The ways in which humans create, listen to, and share music have evolved, much like any other cultural practice. However, technological advancement has accelerated the pace and expanded the reach of cultural change. The technologies discussed in this book have had—and will continue to have—direct implications for vocal practices and musical preferences. For instance, the rise of electromechanical amplification of the voice (along with improved microphone design) in the early twentieth century led to a shift in singing style and vocal techniques. Audio technology enabled singers to be heard by large audiences with less physical effort, allowing them to explore aspects of their voices such as timbre and resonance. Freed from the demanding European operatic techniques that were required for unamplified concerts, mid-twentieth-century artists like Bing Crosby and Frank Sinatra developed the more intimate crooning style (Chanan 1995).

Today, musicians are exploring new possibilities through AI voice technologies, codifying embodied human vocal production and communicative physical gestures as algorithms and expressiveness parameters. What remains unchanged is that most of the singing we hear is electronically mediated. For over a century, people have been listening to our favorite singers' recordings, broadcasts, and concert performances through transducers—speakers, amplifiers, and headphones—making the electronic mediation of human vocal sound not only common but ubiquitous. The synthesized voices discussed in this book sound convincing to my ear because I am accustomed to hearing polished voices, crafted in recording studios, delivering consistent performances in established musical genres. However, in a face-to-face setting, if a friend opened her mouth and a Vocaloid or AI-synthesized vocal sound emerged, I would be immediately plunged into the depths of the uncanny valley. At this stage of technological development, it is still easy to distinguish between the sound emerging from a co-present, embodied human's vocal apparatus, and the sound coming from an electrically powered speaker.

Yet the tools and techniques we choose for creating and consuming art inevitably shape the results—and by extension, the aesthetic values of creators and their communities. This includes decisions about design and use of technological tools. As influential music software developer Miller Puckette observes: "In choosing which shortcuts to provide, the software developer nudges the artist towards a particular set of choices" (Puckette 2023: 28). While using electronic and digital tools, including artificial intelligence, to synthesize singing voices enables the exploration of vast new territories of aesthetic expression, every musical choice, whether listening or sounding, inherently excludes other possibilities. And choosing one path implies that the selected option holds greater value than those left behind. For instance, opting to create music with a synthesized voice means consciously deciding not to sing myself. What will the implications of these new choices be? How will singing through another person's voice, as enabled by live vocal timbre transfer, affect my relationship with my own embodied voice? More broadly, what impact will these changes have on musical practices and the music industry?

These are difficult questions to answer definitively, but they are crucial to consider as technology continues to evolve at an accelerating pace. As Jennifer Edmond notes, "Cultural practices naturally adapt and change over time, and technologies have always been part of this process. However, there is a fine line between enabling cultural change and effecting a change that individuals and groups have little choice or knowledge about" (Edmond 2023). The more powerful the technology becomes, the more parameters must be automated—meaning those parameters are removed from the direct control of human users. The more automation involved, the harder it becomes to choose, or even to ascertain what choices are being made for us.

4.5.2 Ado: Miku's Apprentice

Japanese pop sensation Ado started her career as a small child, singing along with Hatsune Miku. The influence of Vocaloid culture is also the inspiration for her decision to remain anonymous. She now performs massive audiences from the shadows, her face purposely obscured and her personal identity protected. While projecting an anime avatar onstage, Ado's vocal skills seem decidedly human—at least for the time being—as she insists on the uniqueness and irreplaceability of embodied human singing.

It has been over a decade since Vocaloid made it possible to synthesize human-sounding singing—although as producers like kyaami illustrate, it required human skill and painstaking effort to create convincing output. In the mid-2020s, products such as VOCALOID:AI promise (or threaten, depending on your perspective) to make it impossible to know whether any transduced voice originated from a human body. But as bands like Yellow Magic Orchestra showed through their use of musical vocoders, human personhood and its sonic expression can be both exuberant and contentious. We may choose to enjoy the sounds of synthesized voices as magical kin; at the same time, we can also decide that each embodied human's song is something unique and valuable. Protecting each person's right to their own voice is not a new struggle, but it is made surprisingly literal by current trends in AI singing voice synthesis. As Ado herself puts it: "There are some things only a human can do" (Ado qtd. in Robson 2024).

References

Ace Studio: AI Singing Voice Generator. 2023. Website. https://acestudio.ai

AI and Music—Holly Herndon Presents Holly+ feat. Maria Arnal, Tarta Relena and Matthew Dryhurst. 2022. *Sónar Festival*. YouTube. Accessed 21 January 2025. https://www.youtube.com/watch?v=Wk6T2WmhuJw

Ando, Kazuhiro. 2024. How Should Voices Be Legally Protected in the Age of AI? *Yuèdàn fǎxué zázhì* 346: 171–187.

Arekara—NHK Supesharu Baajon (AI Kashō) [Ever Since Then—NHK Special Version (AI Singing)]. 2019. *Hibari Misora Kōshiki YouTube Channeru*. YouTube. Accessed 25 July 2020. https://www.youtube.com/watch?v=rNDWvN5x4Sc

Artificial Intelligence Recreates Deceased Korean Superstar. 2021. *SUBUSUNEWS*. YouTube. Accessed 20 January 2025. https://www.youtube.com/watch?v=WwUHX7oD_ak

Audimee: Unlimited Vocals, Creative Freedom. 2023. https://audimee.com

Bae, Gawon. 2021. South Korea Has Used AI to Bring a Dead Superstar's Voice Back to the Stage, But Ethical Concerns Abound. *CNN*. Accessed 20 January 2025. https://edition.cnn.com/2021/01/25/asia/south-korea-kim-kwang-seok-ai-dst-hnk-intl/index.html

Bergman, Dave, and Cole Stryker. 2024. What is Backpropagation? *IBM*. Website. Accessed 30 October 2024. https://www.ibm.com/think/topics/backpropagation

Blaauw, Merlijn, and Jordi Bonada. 2017. A Neural Parametric Singing Synthesizer Modeling Timbre and Expression from Natural Songs. In *Sound and Music Computing: Applied Sciences Special Issue*, ed. Tapio Lokki, Stefania Serafin, Meinard Muller, and Vesa Valimaki, 250–272. Basel: MDPI.

Brunt, Shelley, and Amane Kasai. 2024. Misora Hibari in Kōhaku Utagassen: From Modernity to Immortality. In *Handbook of Japanese Music in the Modern Era*, ed. Henry Johnson, 405–422. Leiden: Brill.

Chanan, Michael. 1995. *Repeated Takes: A Short History of Recording and Its Effects on Music*. London: Verso.

Chow, Andrew. 2023a. Grimes: Musician. *Time100 AI*. Accessed 20 April 2024. https://time.com/collection/time100-ai/6309464/grimes/

Chow, Andrew. 2023b. Holly Herndon: Musician. *Time100 AI*. Accessed 20 April 2024. https://time.com/collection/time100-ai/6309468/holly-herndon/

Coalition for Sustainable AI. 2025. Website. Accessed 12 February 2025. https://www.sustainableaicoalition.org/coalition/

Datta, Indira. 2019. Chinese Idol Girl Group SNH48 Creates Digital Clones Using AI. *Mobygeek*. Accessed 3 March 2025. https://mobygeek.com/features/chinese-idol-girl-group-snh48-creates-digital-clones-by-ai-1738

Dubey, Abhijit. 2025. Powering the Future: The Energy Shift for Sustainable AI. *World Economic Forum*. Accessed 12 February 2025. https://www.weforum.org/stories/2025/01/the-essential-energy-shift-for-sustainable-genai/

Edmond, Jennifer. 2023. A Quantified Quickening: Data, AI, and the Consumption and Composition of Music. In *Artificial Intelligence and Music Ecosystem*, ed. Martin Clancy, 83–92. London: Routledge.

Exhibition-Related Special Showing: AI x Misora Hibari: Arekara (Ever Since Then). 2019. *Mori Art Museum*. Website. Accessed 20 February 2020. https://www.mori.art.museum/en/exhibitions/future_art/08/index.html

Frana, Philip. 2021. Dartmouth AI Conference. In *Encyclopedia of Artificial Intelligence: The Past, Present and Future of AI*, ed. Philip Frana and Michael J. Klein, 105–106. Santa Barbara, CA: ABC-CLIO.

Gibney, Elizabeth. 2025. China's Cheap, Open AI Model DeepSeek Thrills Scientists. *Nature* 638:13–14.

Glynn, Paul. 2025. Artists Release Silent Album in Protest Against AI Using Their Work. *BBC*. Accessed 25 February 2025. https://www.bbc.com/news/articles/cwyd3r62kp5o

Goodfellow, Ian, Yoshua Bengio, and Aaron Courville. 2016. *Deep Learning*. Cambridge, MA: MIT Press.

Grace, Anna. 2019. Yamaha Vocaloid Recreates Voice of Late Singer. *IQ: Live Music Intelligence*. Accessed 22 February 2020. https://www.iq-mag.net/2019/10/yamaha-vocaloid-recreates-voice-of-late-singer/

Grimes. 2023. *Elf.tech*. Website. https://elf.tech/ Accessed 20 April 2024.

Herndon, Holly. 2021. Holly+. Blog Post. Accessed 13 November 2024. https://holly.mirror.xyz/54ds2IiOnvthjGFkokFCoaI4EabytH9xjAYy1irHy94

Hogan, Mark. 2020. What does JAY-Z's Fight Over Audio Deepfakes Mean for the Future of AI Music? *Pitchfork*. Accessed 20 April 2024. https://pitchfork.com/thepitch/what-does-jay-zs-fight-over-audio-deepfakes-mean-for-the-future-of-ai-music/

Holly Herndon—Eternal (Official Video). 2019. *Holly Herndon*. YouTube. Accessed 13 November 2024. https://www.youtube.com/watch?v=r4sROgbaeOs

Holly Herndon Shares Birthing PROTO. 2019. Dir. Theresa Baumgartner and Zoya Bassi. Film. Accessed 15 November 2024. https://4ad.com/news/10/9/2019/sharesbirthingprotodocumentary

Hono, Yukiya, Shumma Murata, Kazuhiro Nakamura, Kei Hashimoto, Keiichiro Oura, Yoshihiko Nankaku and Keiichi Tokuda. 2018. Recent Development of the DNN-based Singing Voice Synthesis System—Sinsy. In *SPSIPA Annual Summit and Conference Hawaii.* Conference Proceedings.

Jing, Meng. 2018. Chinese Girl Idol Group SNH48 Creates Digital Clones Built by AI. *South China Morning Post.* 25 December 2018. Accessed 22 February 2025. https://www.scmp.com/tech/start-ups/article/2179375/chinese-girl-idol-group-creates-digital-clones-built-ai

Kits AI: ElevenLabs for AI Music and AI Singing. 2024. https://www.kits.ai/blog/elevenlabs

Lo, Kinling. 2025. China's AI Frenzy: DeepSeek is Already Everywhere—Cars, Phones, Even Hospitals. *Rest of the World.* Accessed 16 March 2025. https://restofworld.org/2025/china-embeds-deepseek-ai-in-everything/

Merritt, Rick. 2022. What is a Transformer Model? *NVIDIA.* Blog. Accessed 7 February 2025. https://blogs.nvidia.com/blog/what-is-a-transformer-model/

Milmo, Dan, and Alex Hern. 2024. As the AI World Gathers in Seoul, Can an Accelerating Industry Balance Progress Against Safety? *The Guardian.* Accessed 18 May 2024. https://www.theguardian.com/technology/article/2024/may/18/ai-seoul-global-summit-safety-openai-meta

Moses, Lucia. 2024. The AI Power List: The Most Powerful People in Artificial Intelligence *Business Insider.* Accessed 21 February 2025. https://www.businessinsider.com/holly-herndon-ai-music-art-ai-power-list-2024

Narayanan, Arvind, and Sayash Kapoor. 2024. *AI Snake Oil.* Princeton, NJ: Princeton UP.

New Coalition Aims to Put Artificial Intelligence on a More Sustainable Path. 2025. UN Environment Programme. Website. Accessed 12 February 2025. https://www.unep.org/news-and-stories/press-release/new-coalition-aims-put-artificial-intelligence-more-sustainable-path

New Developed AI Synthesis Engine Produces Natural, Richly Expressive Vocals. 2022. *Yamaha: Make Waves.* Website. Accessed 1 December 2023. https://www.yamaha.com/en/news_release/2022/22101301/

Nishimura, Masanari, Kei Hashimoto, Keiichiro Oura, Yoshihiko Nankaku, and Keiichi Tokuda. 2016. Singing Voice Synthesis Based on Deep Neural Networks. *Interspeech San Francisco.* Conference Proceedings. https://doi.org/10.21437/Interspeech.2016-1027

ObEN Collaborates with SNH48 to Create World's First PAI/Human Music Video. 2018. *Global News Wire.* Accessed 3 March 2025. https://www.globenewswire.com/news-release/2018/12/27/1678626/0/en/ObEN-Collaborates-With-SNH48-to-Create-World-s-First-PAI-Human-Music-Video.html

Pequeño IV, Antonio. 2023. Grimes Helps Artists Distribute Songs Using Her AI Voice—If They Split Royalties. Here's How It Works. *Forbes*. Accessed 4 June 2024. https://www.forbes.com/sites/antoniopequenoiv/2023/06/12/grimes-helps-artists-distribute-songs-using-her-ai-voice%2D%2Dif-they-pay-royalties-heres-how-it-works/

Puckette, Miller. 2023. What Do Music Software Developers Do? In *Artificial Intelligence and Music Ecosystem*, ed. Martin Clancy, 24–34. London: Routledge.

Ren, Yi, Xu Tan, Tao Qin, Jian Luan, Zhou Zhao and Tie-Yan Liu. 2020a. DeepSinger: Singing Voice Synthesis with Data Mined from the Web. *KDD2020 [Knowledge Discovery and Data Mining 2020] Virtual Conference Proceedings*. Association for Computing Machinery Virtual Event, California, USA. https://doi.org/10.1145/3394486.340324

Ren, Yi, Xu Tan, Tao Qin, Jian Luan, Zhou Zhao, and Tie-Yan Liu. 2020b. DeepSinger: Singing Voice Synthesis with Data Mined from the Web. Website. Accessed 12 December 2024. https://speechresearch.github.io/deepsinger/

Robinson, Kristin. 2023. What an Anonymous Artist Taught Us About the Future of AI in Music. *Billboard* 135 (16): 42.

Robson, Daniel. 2024. 'I Express Purely Through My Songs and Silhouette': Ado, the Platinum-selling Pop Star with a Secret Identity. *The Guardian*. Uploaded 11 March 2024. Accessed 11 March 2024. https://www.theguardian.com/music/2024/mar/11/ado-platinum-selling-pop-star-secret-identity-troxy-london

Romo, Vanessa. 2023. Grimes Invites Fans to Make Songs with an AI-generated Version of Her Voice. *National Public Radio*. Uploaded 24 April 2023. Accessed 4 June 2024. https://www.npr.org/2023/04/24/1171738670/grimes-ai-songs-voice

Russell, Stuart, and Peter Norvig. 2021. *Artificial Intelligence: A Modern Approach*. 4th ed. Hoboken, NJ: Pearson.

Scharf, Zach. 2025. Scarlett Johansson Slams AI Video of Celebrities Fighting Kanye West's Antisemitism: 'We Must Call Out the Misuse of AI, No Matter Its Messaging'. *Variety*. Accessed 17 February 2025. https://variety.com/2025/film/news/scarlett-johanasson-ai-video-kanye-west-antisemitism-1236305076/

Seeking Visions for Sustainable AI. 2025. *Nature Machine Intelligence* 7(161). Accessed 1 March 2025. https://www.nature.com/articles/s42256-025-01008-8

Shah, Simmone. 2025. Grimes Celebrates Trailblazers Creating 'Magic' with AI. *Time*. Accessed 11 February 2025. https://time.com/7212518/grimes-ai-time100-impact-awards-dubai/

Silberling, Amanda. 2023. A New Drake x The Weeknd Track Just Blew Up—But It's an AI Fake. *TechCrunch*. Website. Uploaded 23 April 2023. Accessed 7 July 2023. https://techcrunch.com/2023/04/17/uh-oh-an-ai-generated-song-by-drake-and-the-weeknd-went-viral/

Sinsy: HMM/DNN-based Singing Voice Synthesis System. 2024. Website. Accessed 14 January 2025. https://www.sinsy.jp

Spawning Opts Out 78 Million Artworks from AI Training. 2023. Blog. Accessed 12 December 2023. https://spawning.substack.com/p/spawning-opts-out-78-million-artworks

Spawning: Data Governance for Generative AI. 2022. Website. Accessed 12 December 2023. https://spawning.ai/about

Stassen, Murray. 2021. Bit Hit Invests $3.6M in Supertone, an AI Firm that Just Cloned a Dead Superstar's Voice. *Music Business Worldwide*. Accessed 13 January 2025. https://www.musicbusinessworldwide.com/big-hit-invests-3-6m-in-supertone-an-ai-firm-that-just-cloned-a-dead-superstars-voice/

Stassen, Murray. 2022. Over 1,000 Songs with Human-Mimicking AI Vocals Have Been Released by Tencent Music in China. One of Them Has 100M Streams. *Music Business Worldwide*. Accessed 13 January 2025. https://www.musicbusinessworldwide.com/over-1000-songs-human-mimicking-ai-vocals-have-been-released-by-tencent-music-in-china-one-of-them-has-over-100m-streams/

Stryker, Cole and Jim Holdsworth. 2024. What is NLP (Natural Language Processing)? *IBM*. Website. Accessed 30 October 2024. https://www.ibm.com/think/topics/natural-language-processing?

Stryker, Cole and Eda Kavla. 2024. What is Artificial Intelligence (AI)? *IBM*. Website. Actable of contents. Accessed 30 October 2024. https://www.ibm.com/think/topics/artificial-intelligence

Stubbs, Stuart. 2019. Holly Herndon—AI is Not Going to Kill Us; It Might Make Us More Human. *Loud and Quiet*. Accessed 27 September 2024. https://www.loudandquiet.com/interview/holly-herndon/

Suno AI Music: Free AI Music Generator. 2023. https://sunoai-music.com

Tanii, Masato. 2019a. "AI Misora Hibari" wo Sasaeta Gijitsu "Nanairo no Koe" Dō Saigen? Yamaha Gijutsusha ni Kuwashiku Kiita. [How Did the Technology Behind AI Misora Hibari Recreate the Voice of Seven Tone Colors? I Asked Yamaha Engineers for Details]. *IT Media News*. Accessed 19 September 2020. https://www.itmedia.co.jp/news/articles/1910/02/news087_2.html

Tanii, Masato. 2019b. "AI Misora Hibari" no Butaiura "Jōdan de Yatteii Koto Dewanai" Kojin wo Yomigaeraseta Yamaha no Gijitsusha no Omoi [AI Hibari Misora Behind the Scenes—"It's Not Something You Just Do as a Joke": Thoughts of the Yamaha Engineers Who Revived the Late Hibari Misora]. *IT Media News*. Accessed 19 September 2020. https://www.itmedia.co.jp/news/articles/1910/02/news076.html

TuneCore Partners With CreateSafe Using Grimes' Elf.Tech to Facilitate Collaboration Between AI and Self-Releasing Artists. 2023. *TuneCore*. Website. Uploaded 12 June 2023. Accessed 23 January 2024. https://www.tunecore.com/press/tunecore-partners-with-createsafe

Udio Beta. 2023. https://www.udio.com

Voice-Swap. 2023. https://www.voice-swap.ai

What If You Could Sing in Your Favorite Musician's Voice? Holly Herndon. 2022. *TED*. YouTube. https://www.youtube.com/watch?v=5cbCYwgQkTE

Xie, Wendy. 2021. Japanese "Idols" in Trans-cultural Reception: The Case of AKB48. In *The Art of Reception*, ed. Jacobus Bracker and Ann-Kathrin Hubrich, 371–399. Newcastle upon Tyne, UK: Cambridge Scholars Publishing.

Yamaha VOCALOID:AI™ Faithfully Reproduces Singing of Legendary Japanese Vocalist Hibari Misora. 2019. *Yamaha: Make Waves*. Website. Accessed 25 October 2022. https://archive.yamaha.com/en/news_release/2019/19110080l/

Yano, Christine. 2002. *Tears of Longing: Nostalgia and the Nation in Japanese Popular Song*. Cambridge, MA: Harvard UP.

Zaborowski, Rafal. 2025. Virtual (Idol) Audiences: Canon, Fanon, and Multivocality in Vocaloid Cultures. In *The Routledge Companion to Media Audiences*, ed. Annette Hill and Peter Lunt, 222–233. Routledge.

Index[1]

A
AI Hibari, 64, 70, 72, 73
"Ano Subarashii Ai Wo Mō Ichidō," 54
"Arekara," 64, 71
Articulation, 9, 25, 27, 47, 53, 71
Auditory system, 13, 15, 29

B
Behind the Mask, 22–23
Bell Telephone Laboratories, 23–24, 42

C
CANTOR, 48–49
CataRT, 48
CHANT, 46, 47
Character Vocal Series, 2, 51, 56, 57

Concatenative synthesis, 47–49, 52, 57, 74
Consonants, 4, 4n4, 8, 14, 24, 35, 46, 47, 54, 64
Crypton Future Media, 2, 50, 55–57

D
Daisy Bell, 42, 54–55
Daisy Project, 49, 50
Deepfakes, 74, 76
Deep neural networks, 67–69, 71
DeepSinger, 71–72
Diphones, 53
DX7, 56

E
Elf.tech, 76–78
THE END, 52

---

[1] Note: Page numbers followed by 'n' refer to notes.

© The Author(s), under exclusive license to Springer Nature Switzerland AG 2025
G. Jude, *How Vocaloid Works*,
https://doi.org/10.1007/978-3-031-92727-0

F
Filter, 24, 25, 27, 28, 37, 45, 48, 50, 76
Formant, 8, 24, 26–29, 34, 35, 46, 48
Fourier transform, 44–45, 47–49
Frequency, 6–8, 11–15, 24–27, 29, 35, 44, 45, 55
Fujita, Saki, 57–58

G
"The Girl in Byakkoya," 35
Grimes, 76

H
HAL9000, 37, 42
Harmonics, 7–8, 12, 13, 30, 35
Hatsune Miku, 2–5, 22, 49–58, 73, 80
Helmholtz resonators, 12
Herndon, Holly, 69, 75, 77
Hirasawa, Susumu, 35, 50
Holly+, 69–70, 72–78
Horror, 32

I
IBM 7094, 42

K
Kaito, 50, 54, 56
Kelly, John L., 43
Kenmochi, Hideki, 49, 53
Kyaami, 4, 15, 80

L
Large language models, 67, 78
Larynx, 6, 7, 25, 26, 36

Leon, 50, 55–57
Lochbaum, Carol, 43
Lola, 35, 50, 55–57
Lyricos, 47–48

M
Machine learning, 58, 65, 68, 70
"Mahō," 4, 15
Matsutake, Hideki, 22, 50, 54
Meiko, 35, 54
Miriam, 35, 50, 55–57
Misora Hibari, 64, 70

N
Nyquist limit, 43–44

O
Opt out, 76, 78
Oscillator, 24, 25, 28

P
Paprika, 35–37
"Parade," 36
Perceptualization, 29
Physical models, 10, 12, 28, 45, 47

R
Resonance, 7, 8, 23, 25, 29, 30, 35, 36, 50, 79

S
Sampling rate, 44, 52
Sine wave, 12, 24, 45
Sinsy, 68–69

Sound-image asynchrony, 33, 34
Source-filter model, 27–28, 49–50
Spawning, 74–76
Spectral models, 24, 25, 28, 45, 47, 49, 50
Symphony Ihatov, 52

T
Timbre, 7, 12, 23, 30, 37, 46, 49, 50, 50n6, 54, 64, 68–70, 72, 74, 75, 79, 80
Transformer architecture, 67, 71
2001: A Space Odyssey, 37, 42

U
Uncanny valley, 30–34, 72, 79

V
Virtual Soul Vocalists, 56
Vocalization, 3, 5, 6, 9, 14, 26, 28, 32–35, 43, 69
VOCALOID:AI, 64, 70, 73, 80
Vocal tract, 7, 8, 25, 27, 28, 30, 35, 43, 46, 50
Vocoder, 22–25, 28, 34, 43, 55, 80
Vowels, 8, 9, 12, 23, 27, 46, 54, 64

Y
Yellow Magic Orchestra, 22–23, 50, 54, 80

Z
Zero-G, 50, 55–57